MAX AXIOM
AND THE SOCIETY OF SUPER SCIENTISTS

JOURNEYING TO NEW WORLDS

BY NEL YOMTOV

ILLUSTRATED BY DANIEL PEDROSA

CAPSTONE PRESS
a capstone imprint

Published by Capstone Press, an imprint of Capstone.
1710 Roe Crest Drive North Mankato, Minnesota 56003
capstonepub.com

Library of Congress Cataloging-in-Publication Data
Names: Yomtov, Nelson, author. | Pedrosa, Daniel, illustrator.
Title: Journeying to new worlds / by Nel Yomtov ; illustrated by Daniel Pedrosa.
Description: North Mankato, Minnesota : Capstone Press, [2023] | Series: Max Axiom and the Society of Super Scientists | Includes bibliographical references and index. | Audience: Ages 8-11 | Audience: Grades 4-6 |
Summary: "Ever since the first astronauts traveled to space in the 1960s, scientists and engineers have worked hard to learn more about space travel. What kinds of spaceships will people use in the future? How will their needs be met during the long journey between Earth and some distant world? In this nonfiction graphic novel, Max Axiom and the Society of Super Scientists look for the answers to these questions and more as they learn about modern space tourism and the future of space travel"-- Provided by publisher.
Identifiers: LCCN 2021056939 (print) | LCCN 2021056940 (ebook) | ISBN 9781666337037 (hardcover) | ISBN 9781666337044 (paperback) | ISBN 9781666337051 (ebook pdf) | ISBN 9781666337075 (Kindle edition)
Subjects: LCSH: Interplanetary voyages--Juvenile literature. | Space tourism--Juvenile literature. | Outer space--Exploration--Juvenile literature. | Space travel--Comic books, strips, etc. | Graphic novels.
Classification: LCC TL788.7 .Y66 2023 (print) | LCC TL788.7 (ebook) | DDC 919.904--dc23/eng/20220124
LC record available at https://lccn.loc.gov/2021056939
LC ebook record available at https://lccn.loc.gov/2021056940

Editorial Credits
Editor: Aaron Sautter; Designer: Brann Garvey; Media Researcher: Morgan Walters; Production Specialist: Polly Fisher

All internet sites appearing in back matter were available and accurate when this book was sent to press.

Printed and bound in the USA.

TABLE OF CONTENTS

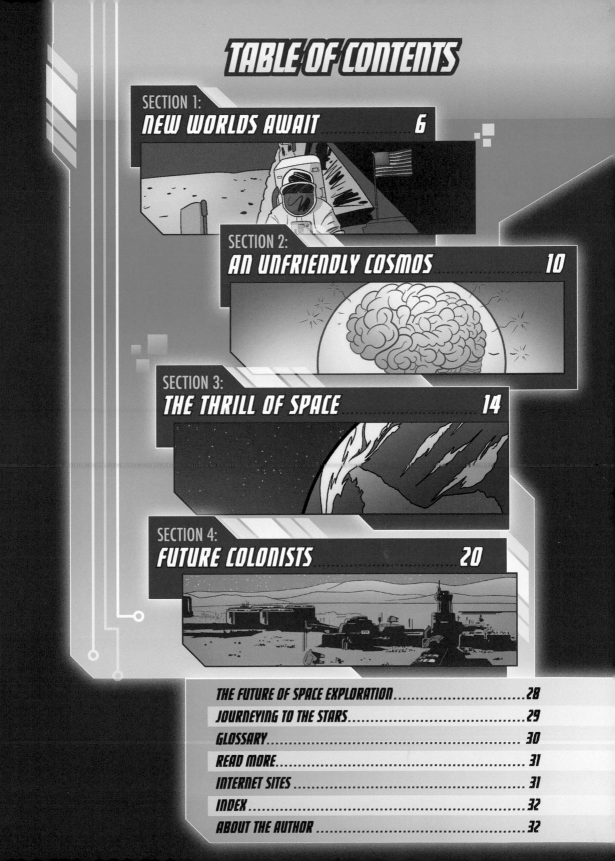

THE SOCIETY OF SUPER SCIENTISTS

MAX AXIOM

After years of study, Max Axiom, the world's first Super Scientist, knew the mysteries of the universe were too vast for one person alone to uncover. So Max created the Society of Super Scientists! Using their superpowers and super-smarts, this talented group investigates today's most urgent scientific and environmental issues and learns about actions everyone can take to solve them.

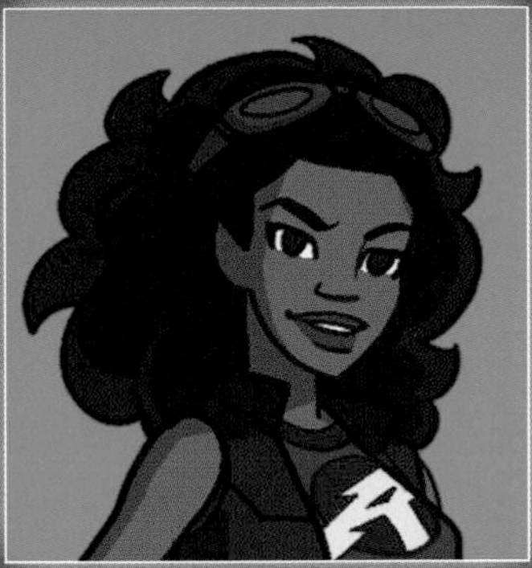

LIZZY AXIOM

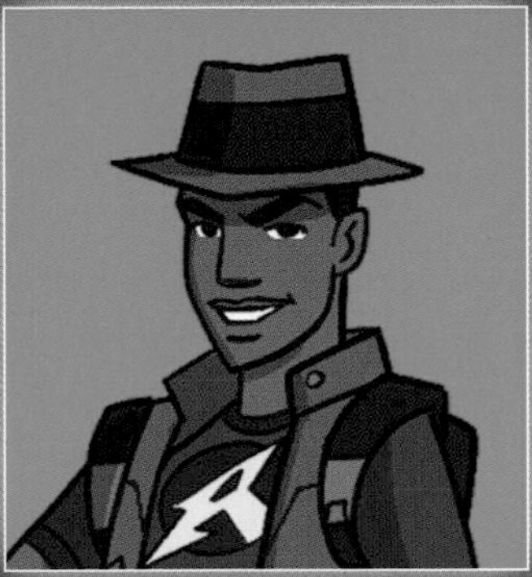

NICK AXIOM

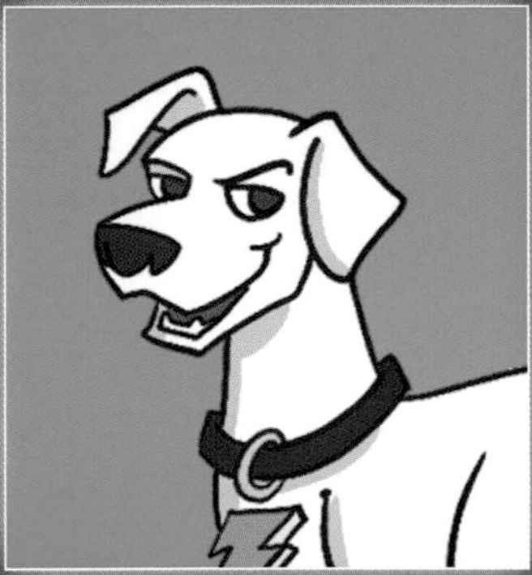

SPARK

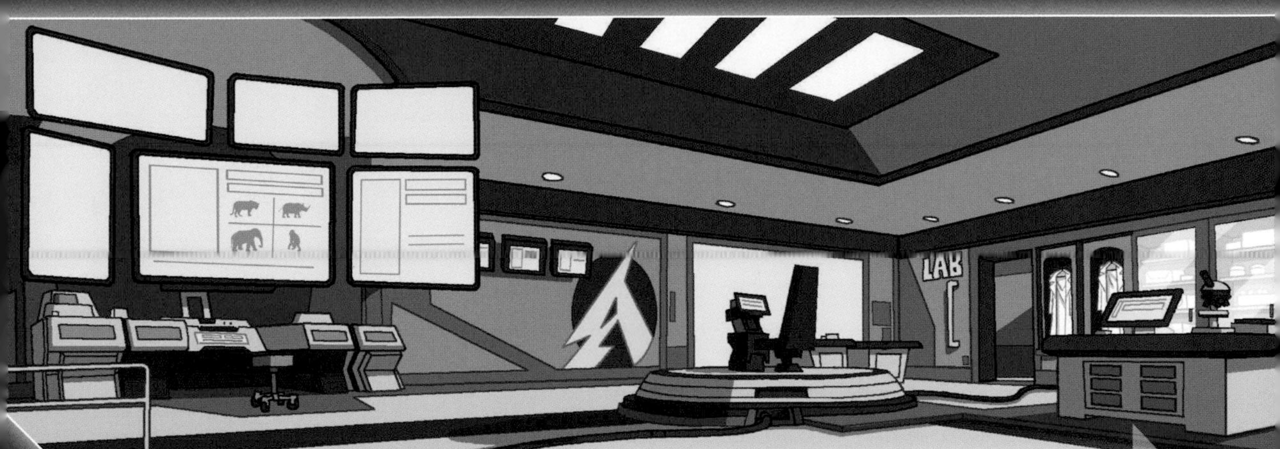
LAB

THE DISCOVERY LAB

Home of the Society of Super Scientists, this state-of-the-art lab houses advanced tools for cutting-edge research and radical scientific innovation. More importantly, it is a space for Super Scientists to collaborate and share knowledge as they work together to tackle any challenge.

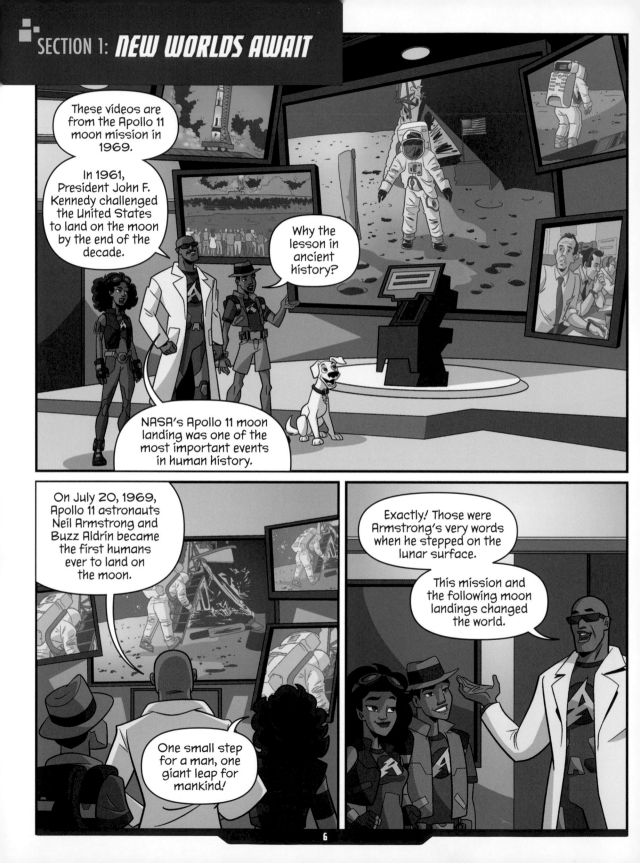

These videos are from the Apollo 11 moon mission in 1969.

In 1961, President John F. Kennedy challenged the United States to land on the moon by the end of the decade.

Why the lesson in ancient history?

NASA's Apollo 11 moon landing was one of the most important events in human history.

On July 20, 1969, Apollo 11 astronauts Neil Armstrong and Buzz Aldrin became the first humans ever to land on the moon.

One small step for a man, one giant leap for mankind!

Exactly! Those were Armstrong's very words when he stepped on the lunar surface.

This mission and the following moon landings changed the world.

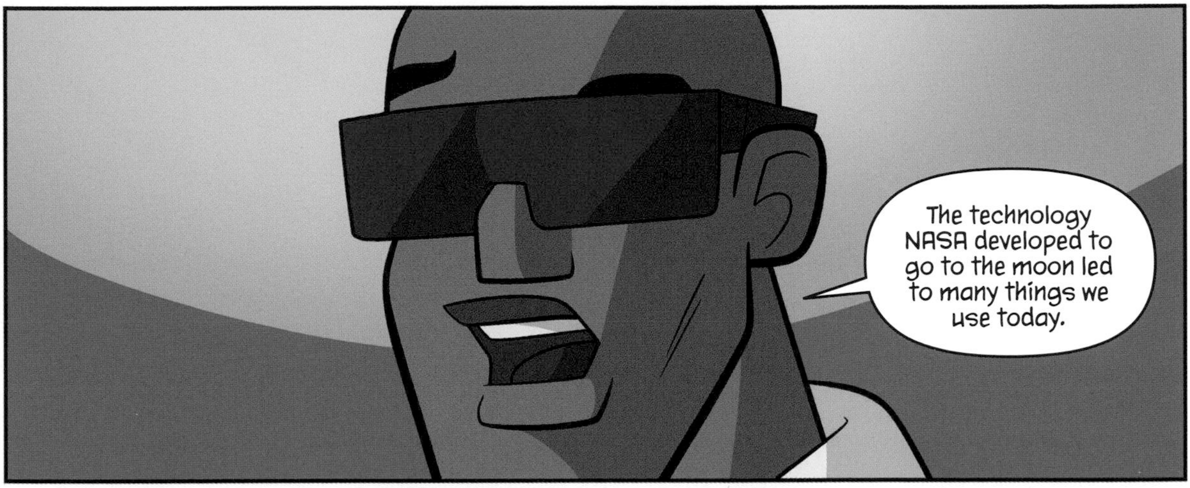
The technology NASA developed to go to the moon led to many things we use today.

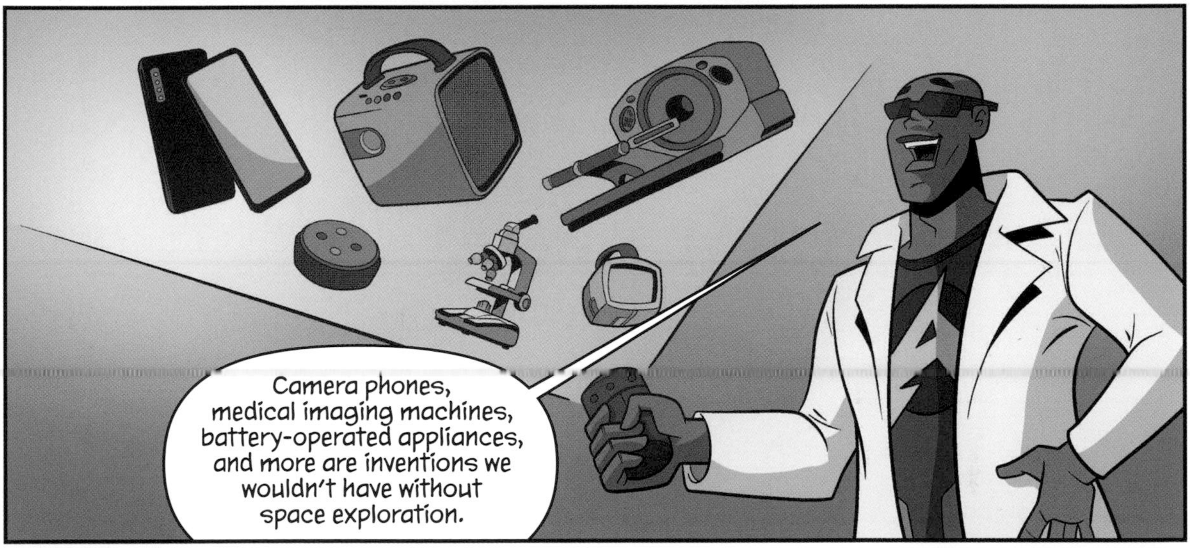
Camera phones, medical imaging machines, battery-operated appliances, and more are inventions we wouldn't have without space exploration.

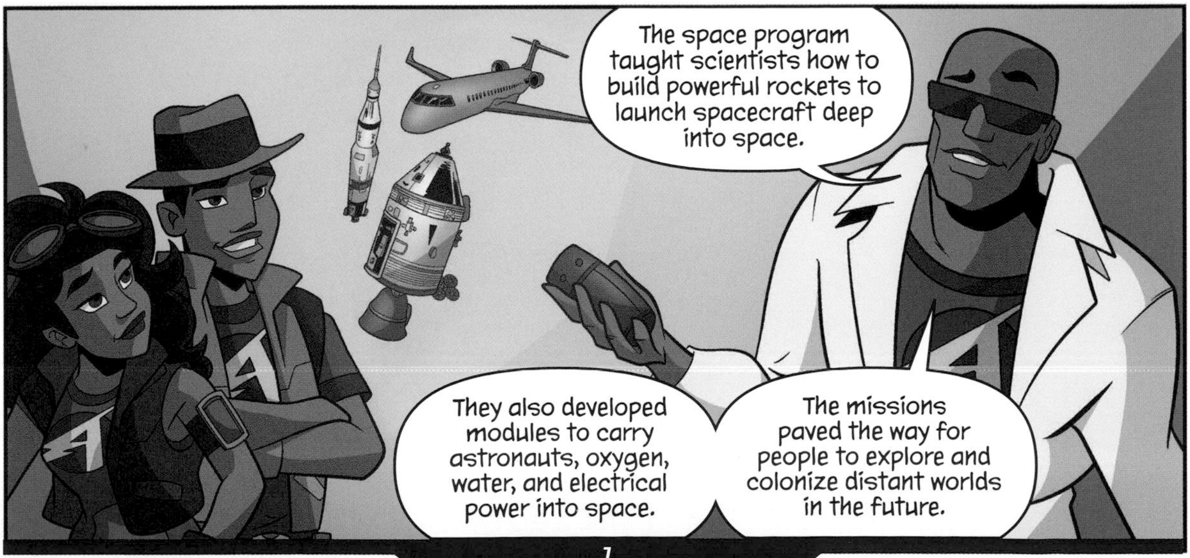
The space program taught scientists how to build powerful rockets to launch spacecraft deep into space.
They also developed modules to carry astronauts, oxygen, water, and electrical power into space.
The missions paved the way for people to explore and colonize distant worlds in the future.

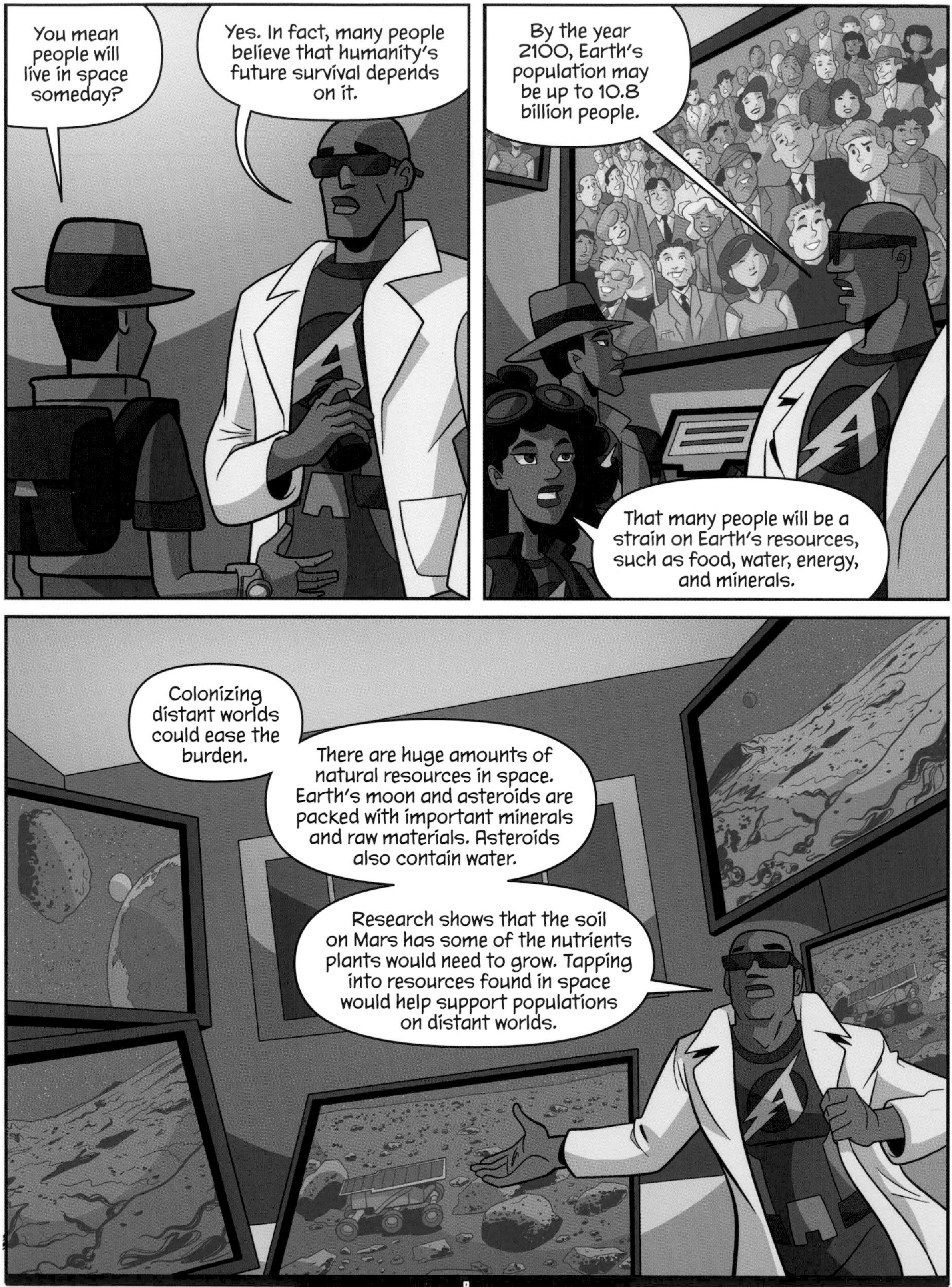
You mean people will live in space someday?
Yes. In fact, many people believe that humanity's future survival depends on it.
By the year 2100, Earth's population may be up to 10.8 billion people.
That many people will be a strain on Earth's resources, such as food, water, energy, and minerals.
Colonizing distant worlds could ease the burden.
There are huge amounts of natural resources in space. Earth's moon and asteroids are packed with important minerals and raw materials. Asteroids also contain water.
Research shows that the soil on Mars has some of the nutrients plants would need to grow. Tapping into resources found in space would help support populations on distant worlds.

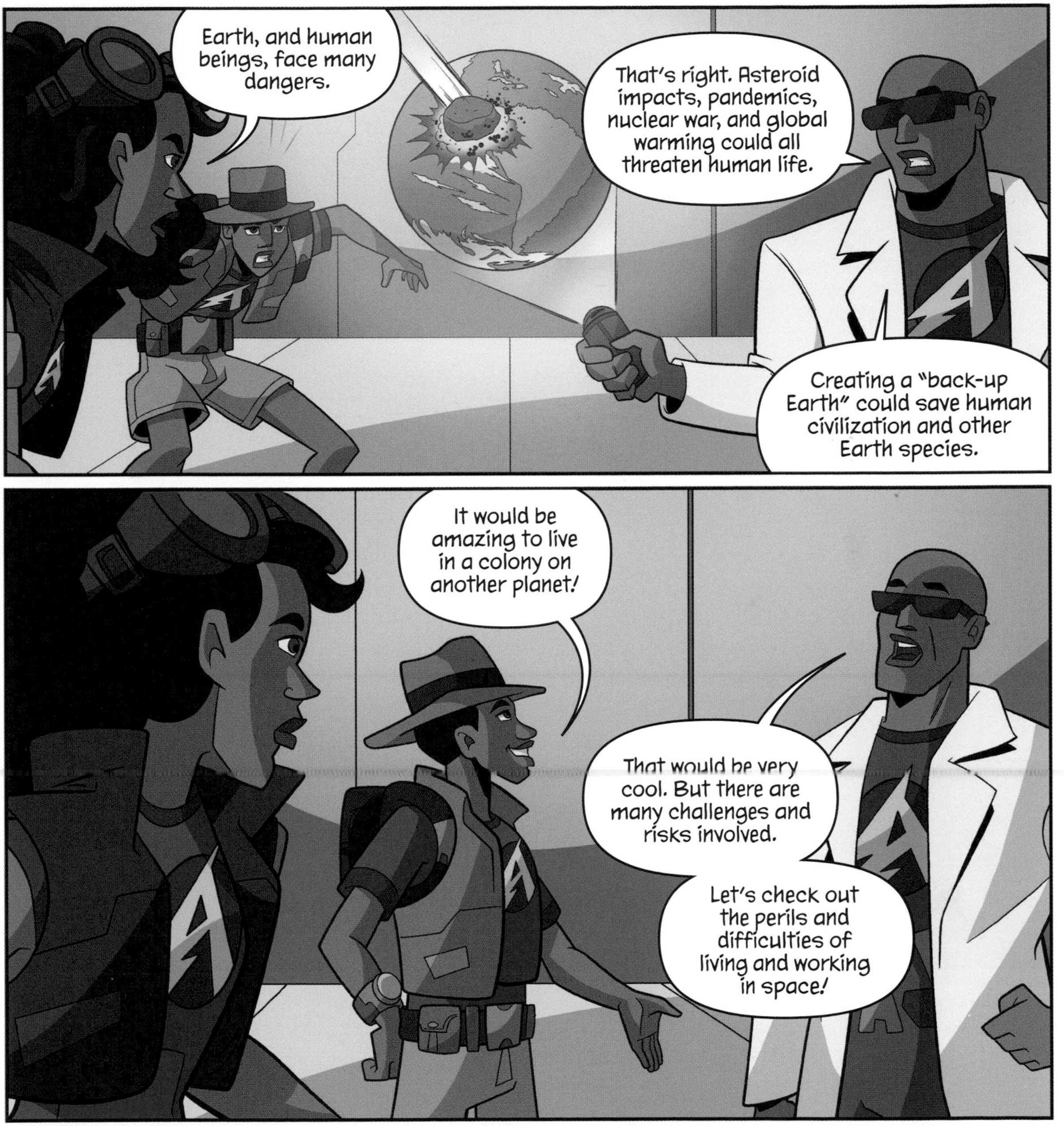
Earth, and human beings, face many dangers.
That's right. Asteroid impacts, pandemics, nuclear war, and global warming could all threaten human life.
Creating a "back-up Earth" could save human civilization and other Earth species.
It would be amazing to live in a colony on another planet!
That would be very cool. But there are many challenges and risks involved.
Let's check out the perils and difficulties of living and working in space!

A BOLD PREDICTION

The first known prediction about a lunar colony dates back nearly 400 years. In 1638, John Wilkins wrote *The Discovery of a World in the Moone*. He claimed, "as soon as the art of flying is found out . . .," humans, " . . . will make one of the first colonies that shall inhabit that other world."

SECTION 2: *AN UNFRIENDLY COSMOS*

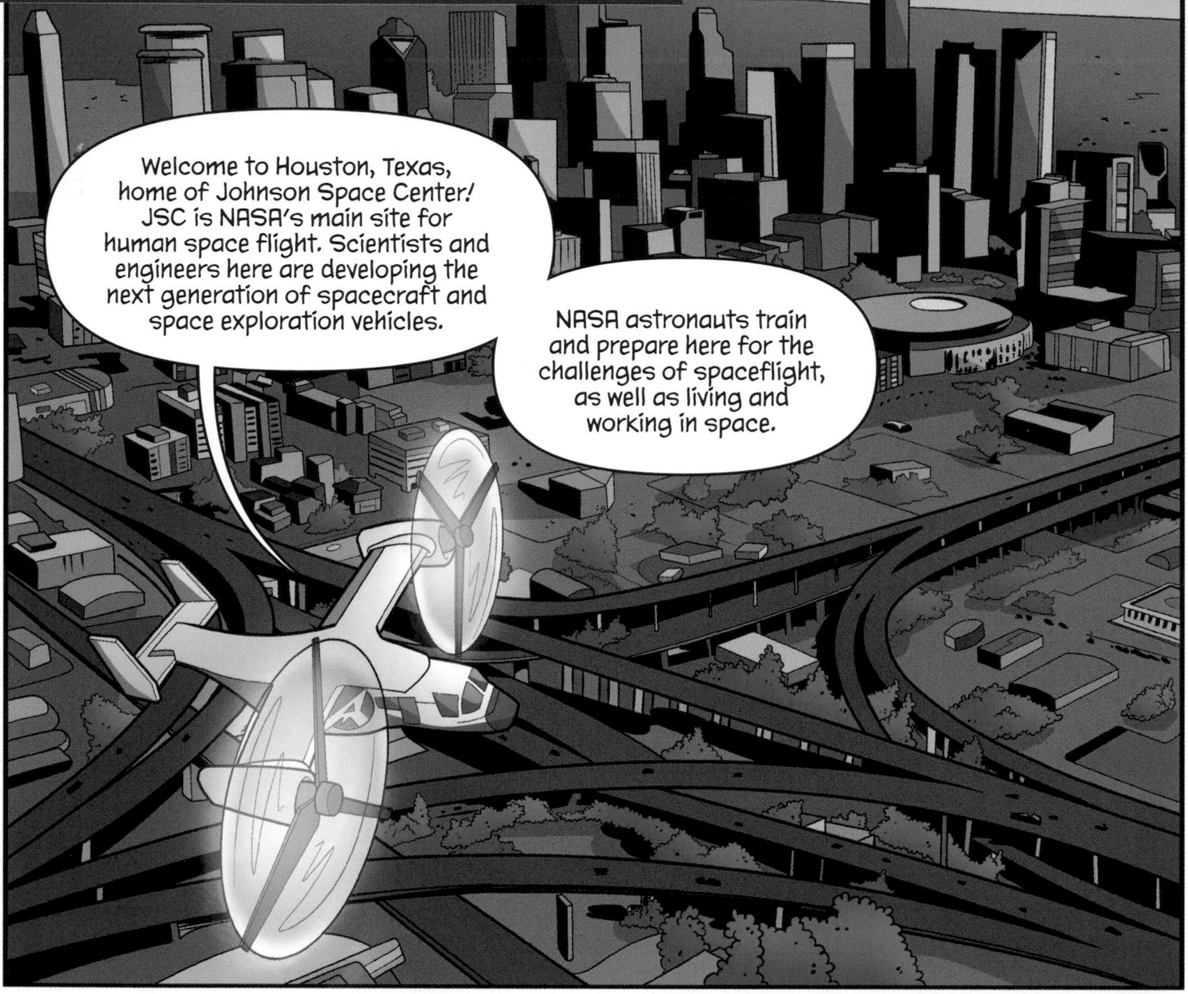
Welcome to Houston, Texas, home of Johnson Space Center! JSC is NASA's main site for human space flight. Scientists and engineers here are developing the next generation of spacecraft and space exploration vehicles.
NASA astronauts train and prepare here for the challenges of spaceflight, as well as living and working in space.

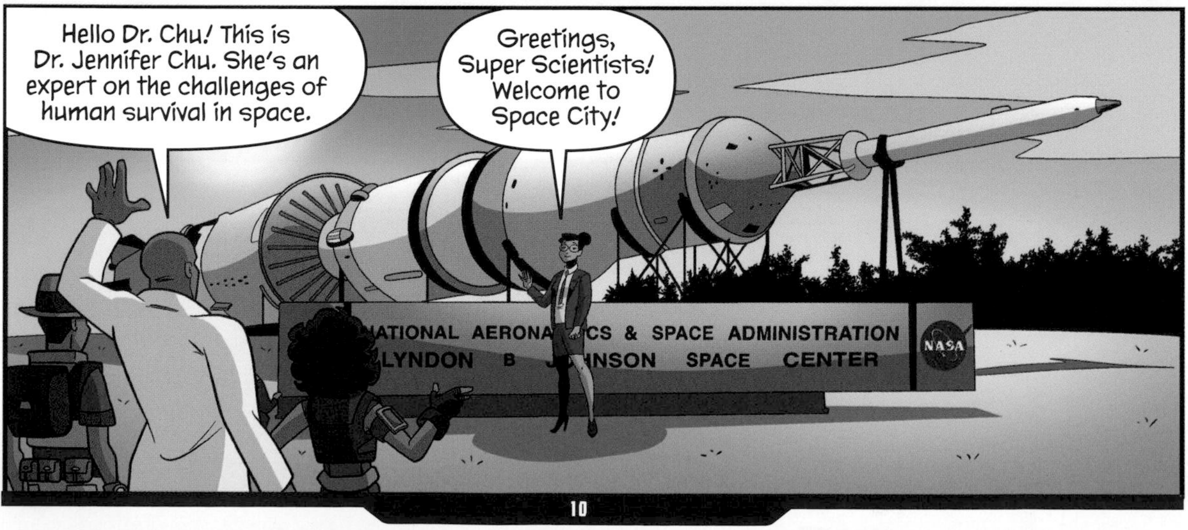
Hello Dr. Chu! This is Dr. Jennifer Chu. She's an expert on the challenges of human survival in space.
Greetings, Super Scientists! Welcome to Space City!
ATIONAL AERONA CS & SPACE ADMINISTRATION
LYNDON B J NSON SPACE CENTER
NASA

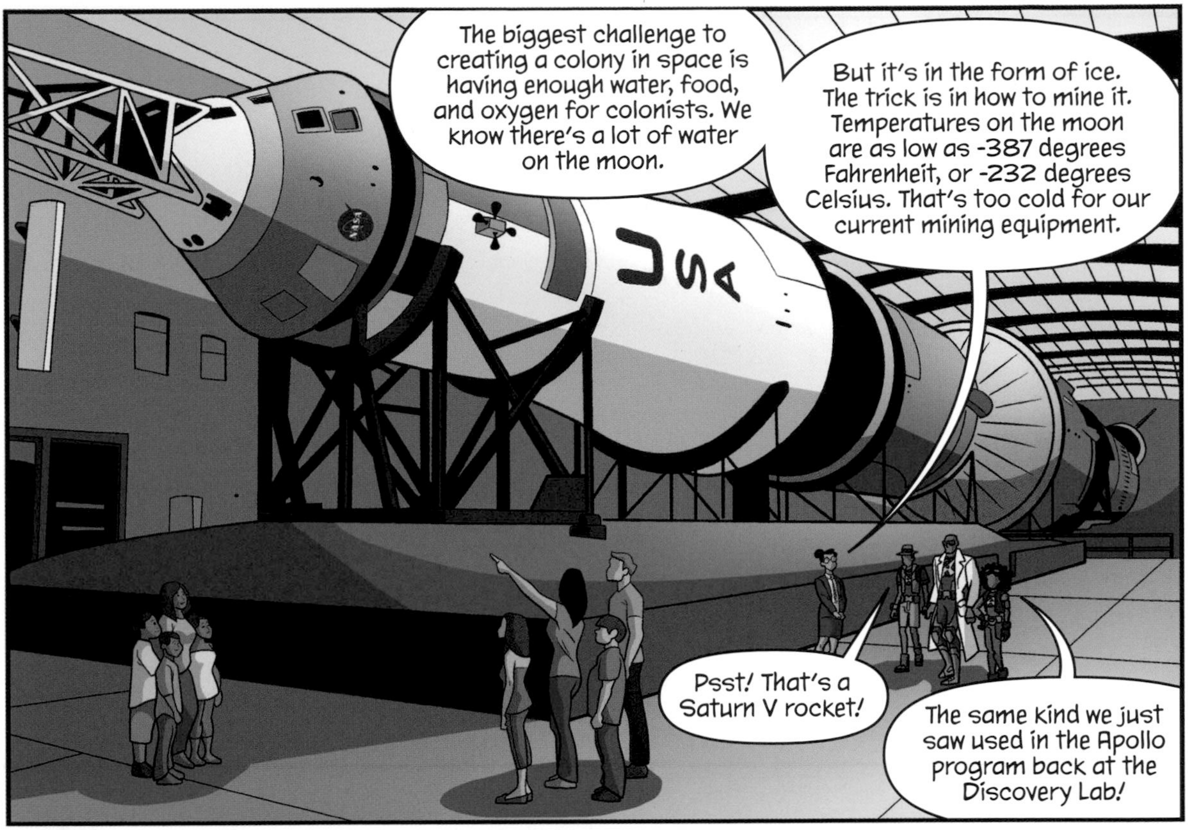
The biggest challenge to creating a colony in space is having enough water, food, and oxygen for colonists. We know there's a lot of water on the moon.
But it's in the form of ice. The trick is in how to mine it. Temperatures on the moon are as low as -387 degrees Fahrenheit, or -232 degrees Celsius. That's too cold for our current mining equipment.
USA
Psst! That's a Saturn V rocket!
The same kind we just saw used in the Apollo program back at the Discovery Lab!

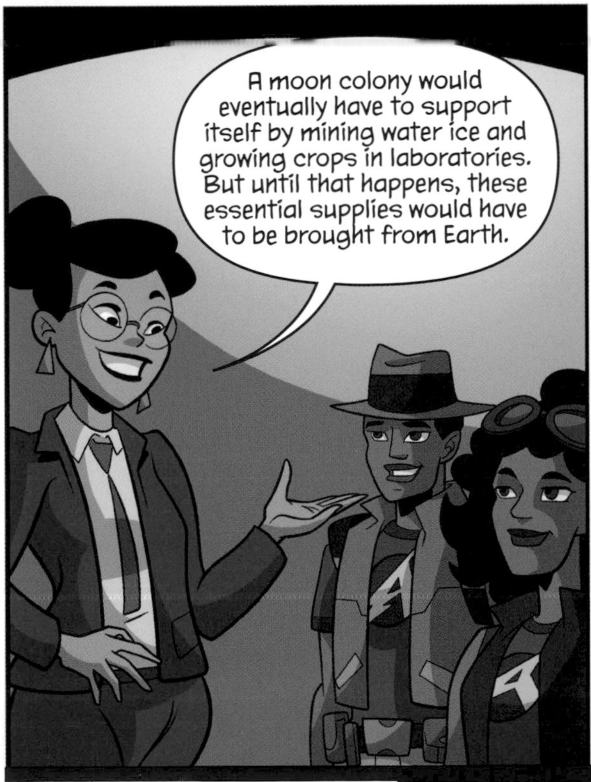
A moon colony would eventually have to support itself by mining water ice and growing crops in laboratories. But until that happens, these essential supplies would have to be brought from Earth.

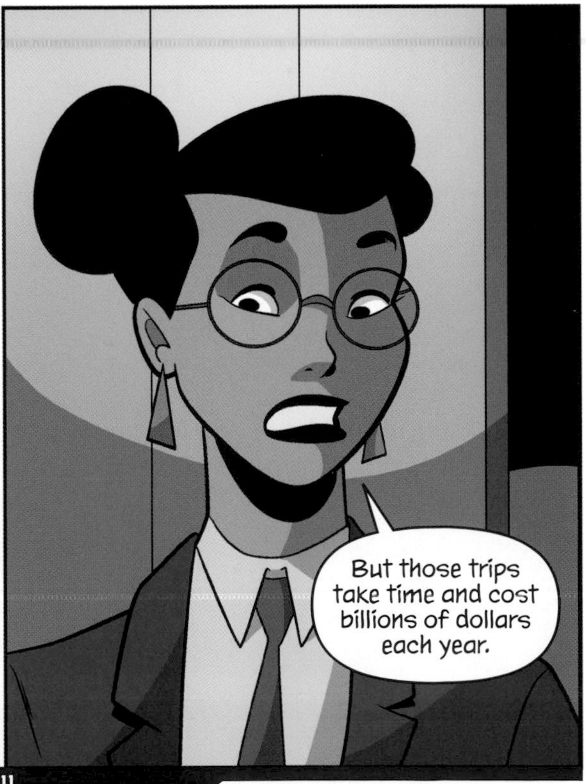
But those trips take time and cost billions of dollars each year.

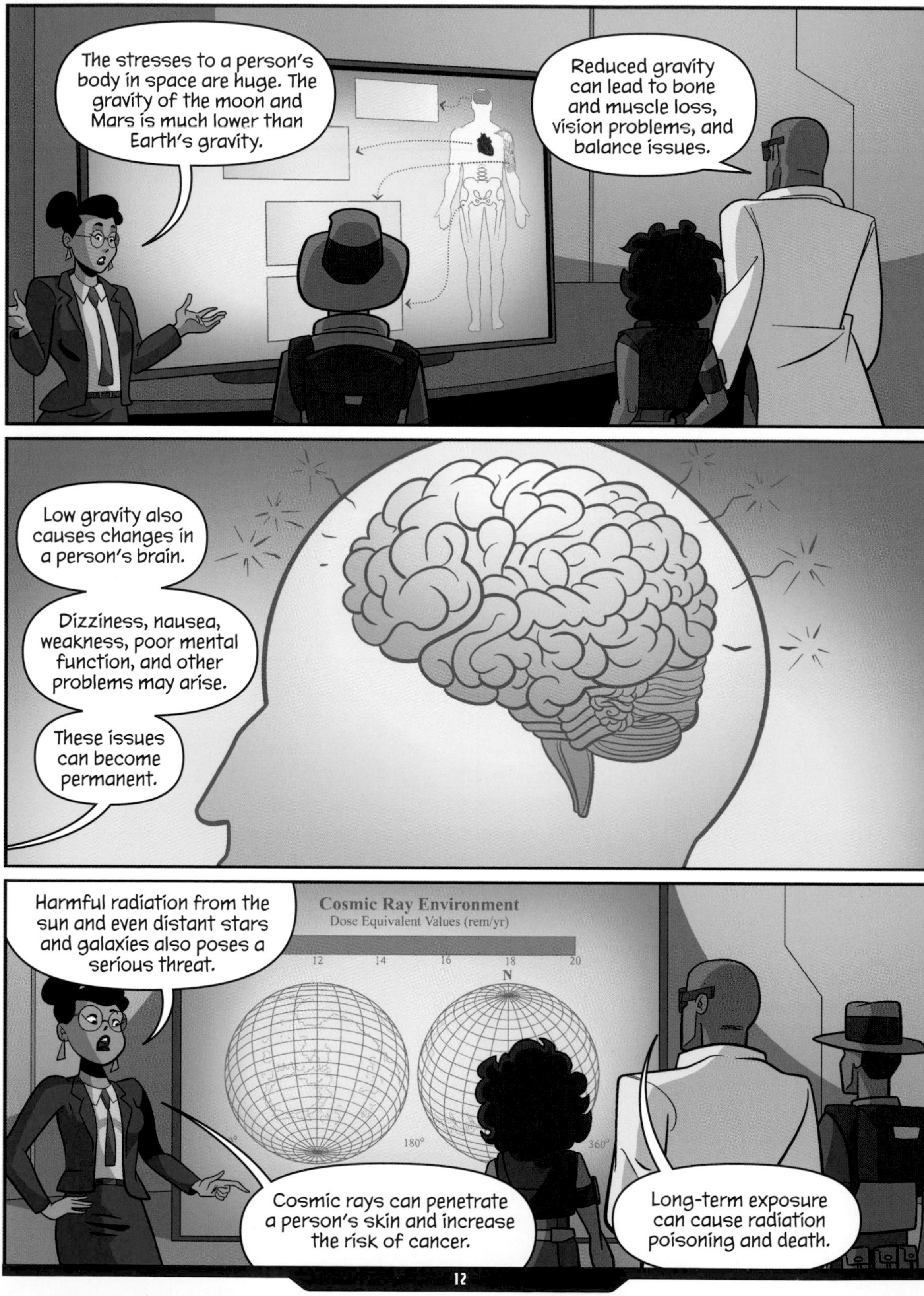

The stresses to a person's body in space are huge. The gravity of the moon and Mars is much lower than Earth's gravity.
Reduced gravity can lead to bone and muscle loss, vision problems, and balance issues.
Low gravity also causes changes in a person's brain.
Dizziness, nausea, weakness, poor mental function, and other problems may arise.
These issues can become permanent.
Harmful radiation from the sun and even distant stars and galaxies also poses a serious threat.
Cosmic Ray Environment
Dose Equivalent Values (rem/yr)
12
14
16
18
20
N
180°
360°
Cosmic rays can penetrate a person's skin and increase the risk of cancer.
Long-term exposure can cause radiation poisoning and death.

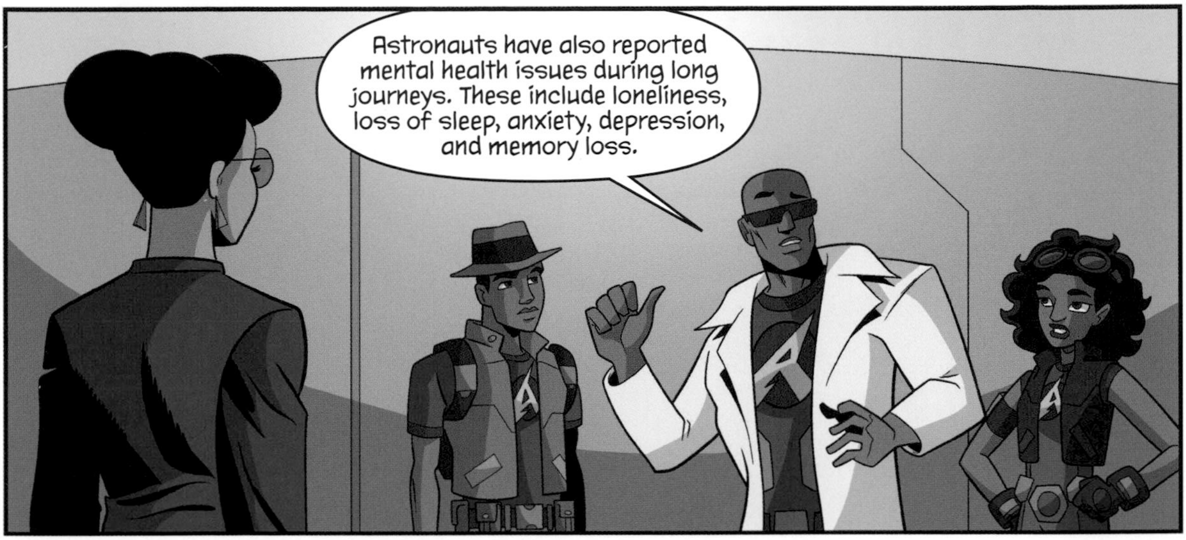
Astronauts have also reported mental health issues during long journeys. These include loneliness, loss of sleep, anxiety, depression, and memory loss.

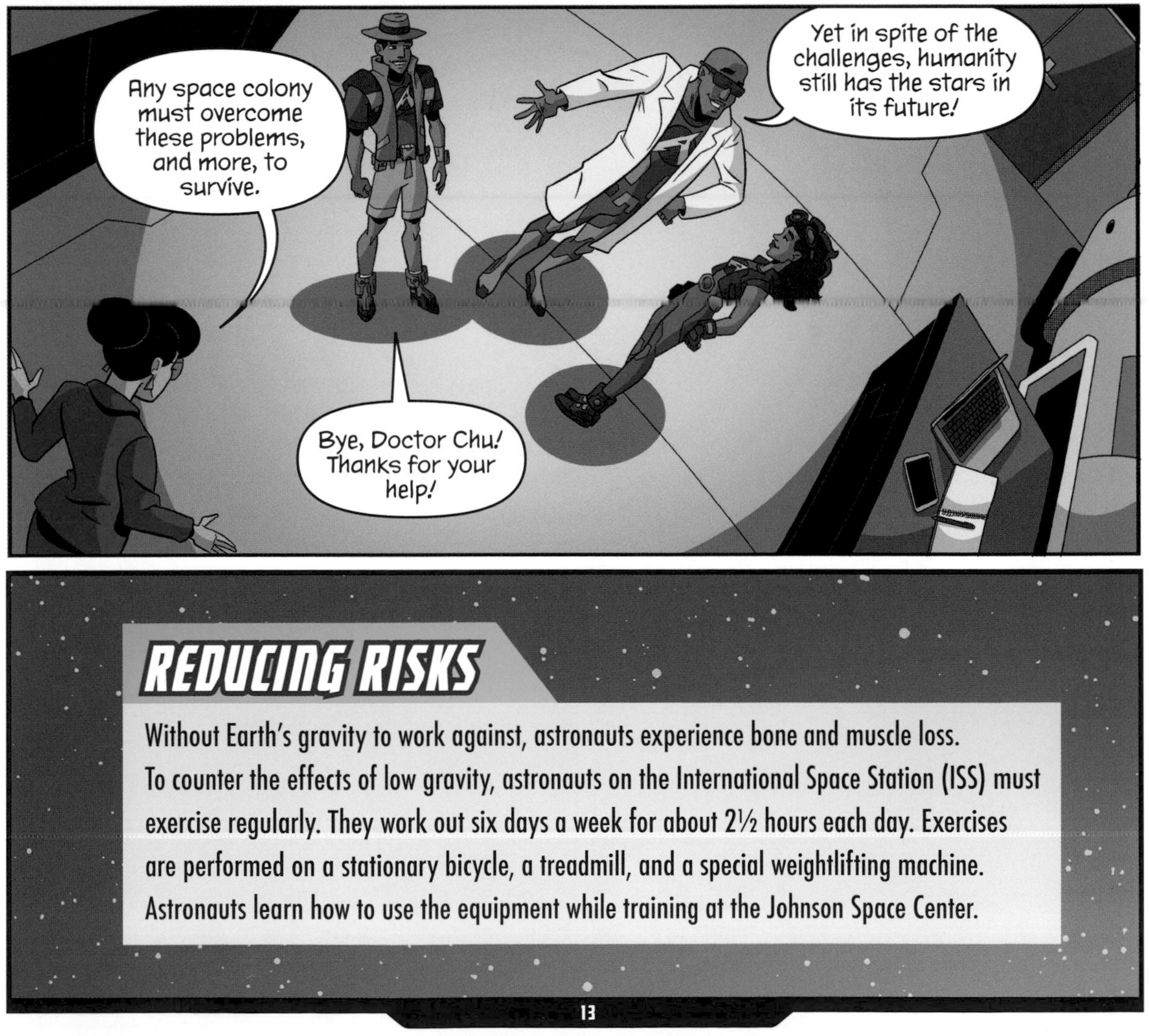
Any space colony must overcome these problems, and more, to survive.
Yet in spite of the challenges, humanity still has the stars in its future!
Bye, Doctor Chu! Thanks for your help!

REDUCING RISKS

Without Earth's gravity to work against, astronauts experience bone and muscle loss. To counter the effects of low gravity, astronauts on the International Space Station (ISS) must exercise regularly. They work out six days a week for about 2½ hours each day. Exercises are performed on a stationary bicycle, a treadmill, and a special weightlifting machine. Astronauts learn how to use the equipment while training at the Johnson Space Center.

SECTION 3: *THE THRILL OF SPACE*

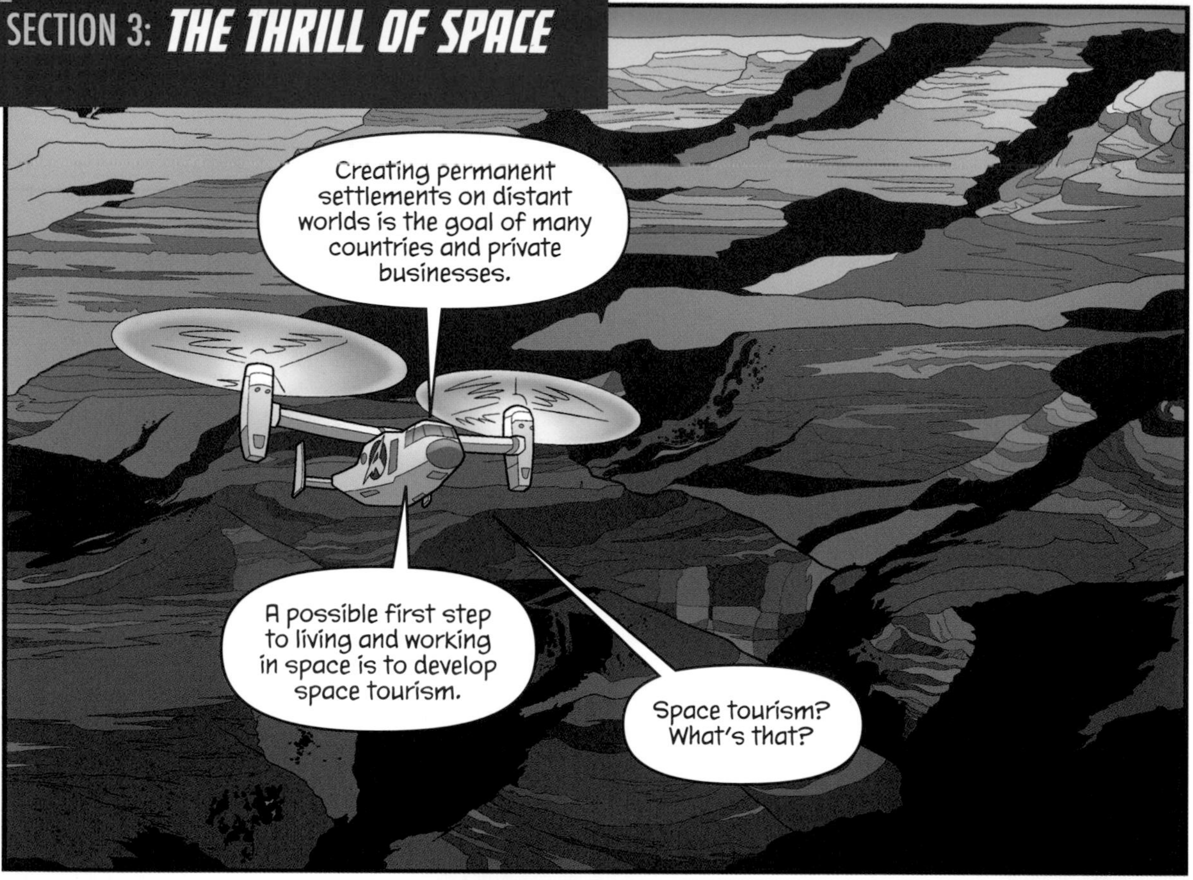

Creating permanent settlements on distant worlds is the goal of many countries and private businesses.
A possible first step to living and working in space is to develop space tourism.
Space tourism? What's that?

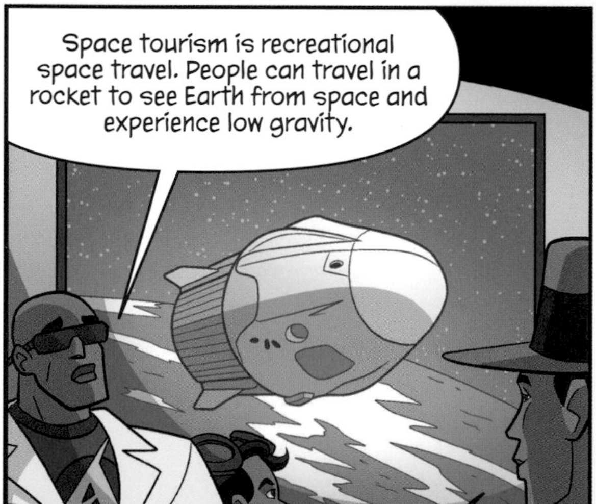

Space tourism is recreational space travel. People can travel in a rocket to see Earth from space and experience low gravity.
Count me in! Where do I sign up?

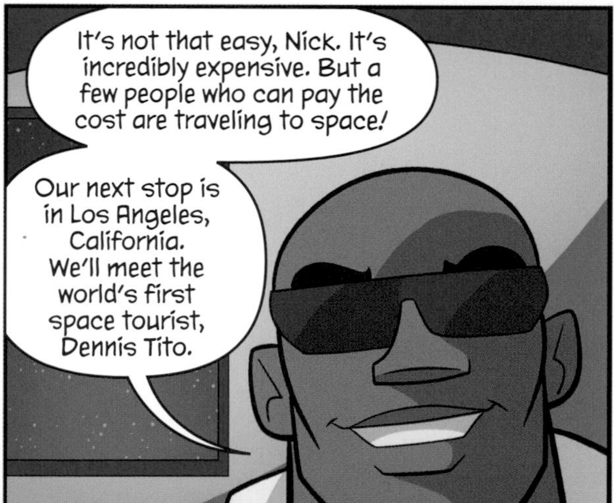

It's not that easy, Nick. It's incredibly expensive. But a few people who can pay the cost are traveling to space!
Our next stop is in Los Angeles, California. We'll meet the world's first space tourist, Dennis Tito.

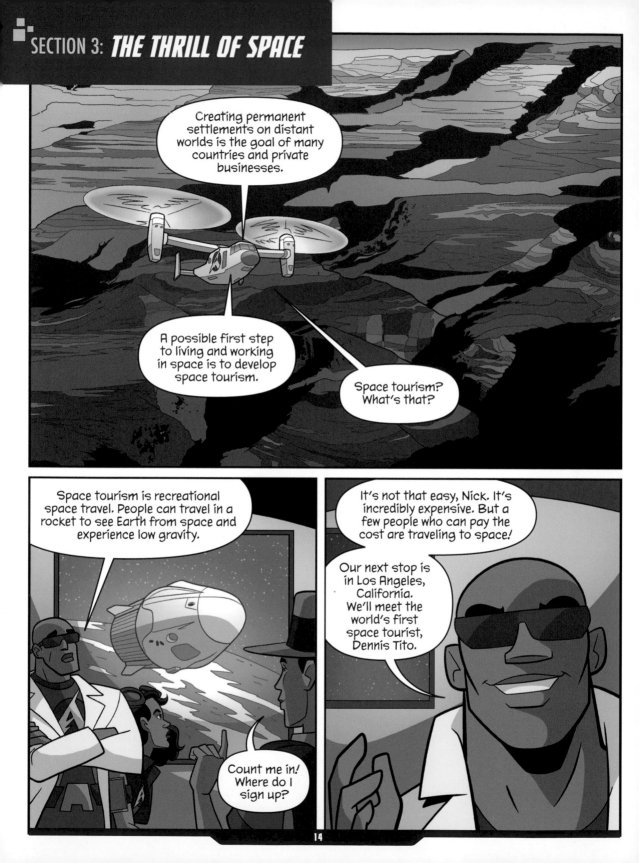

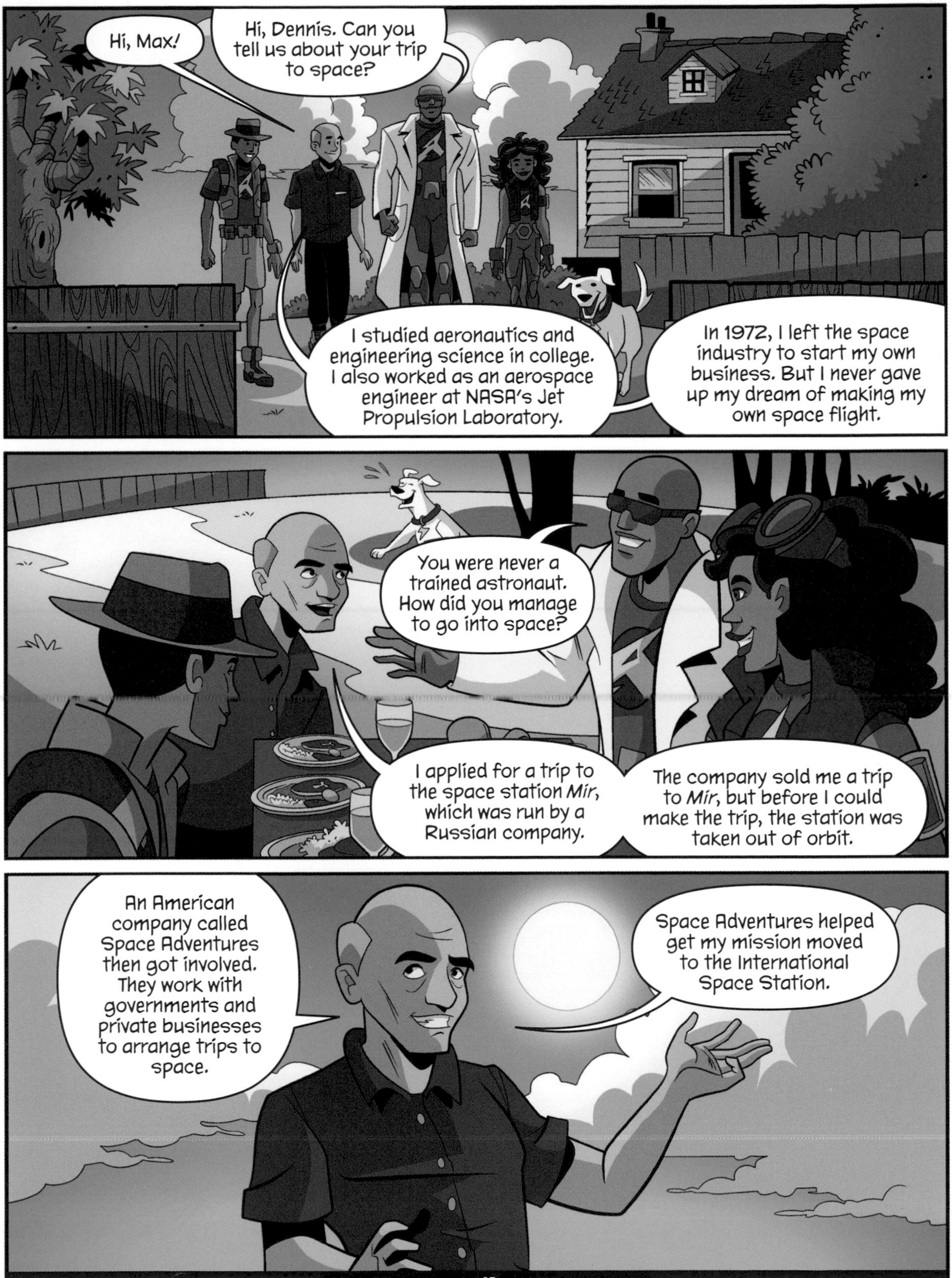
Hi, Max!
Hi, Dennis. Can you tell us about your trip to space?
I studied aeronautics and engineering science in college. I also worked as an aerospace engineer at NASA's Jet Propulsion Laboratory.
In 1972, I left the space industry to start my own business. But I never gave up my dream of making my own space flight.
You were never a trained astronaut. How did you manage to go into space?
I applied for a trip to the space station *Mir*, which was run by a Russian company.
The company sold me a trip to *Mir*, but before I could make the trip, the station was taken out of orbit.
An American company called Space Adventures then got involved. They work with governments and private businesses to arrange trips to space.
Space Adventures helped get my mission moved to the International Space Station.

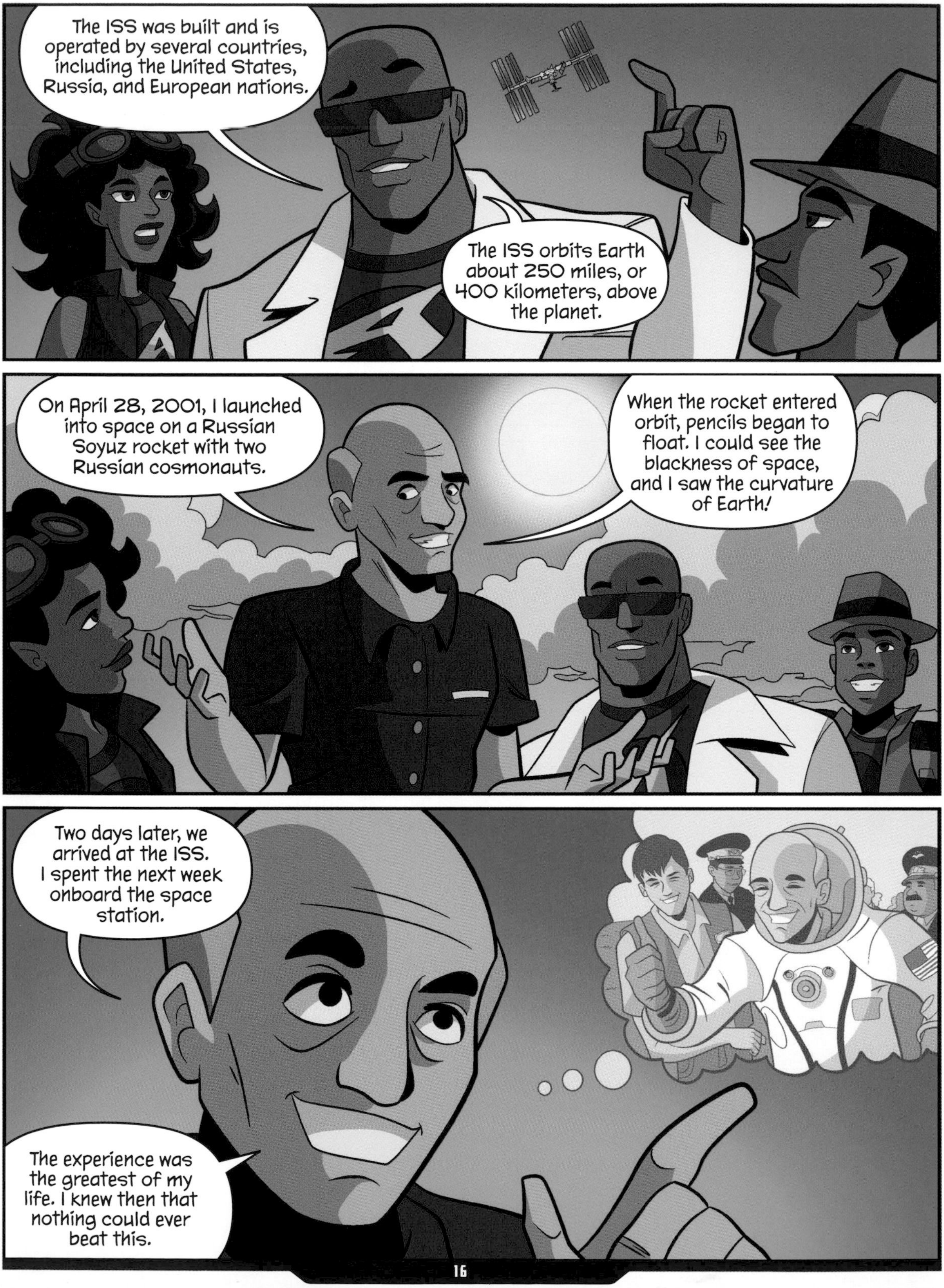
The ISS was built and is operated by several countries, including the United States, Russia, and European nations.
The ISS orbits Earth about 250 miles, or 400 kilometers, above the planet.
On April 28, 2001, I launched into space on a Russian Soyuz rocket with two Russian cosmonauts.
When the rocket entered orbit, pencils began to float. I could see the blackness of space, and I saw the curvature of Earth!
Two days later, we arrived at the ISS. I spent the next week onboard the space station.
The experience was the greatest of my life. I knew then that nothing could ever beat this.

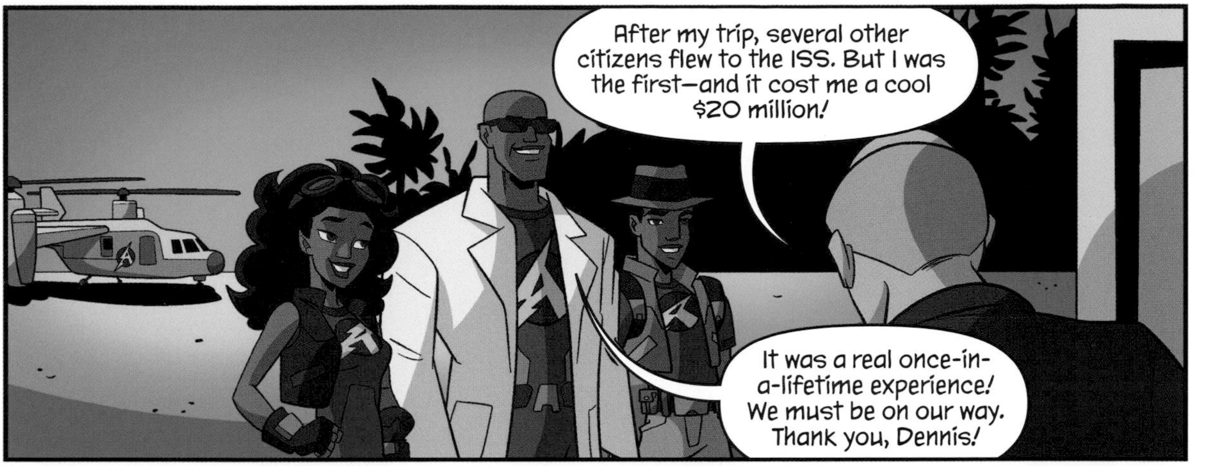
After my trip, several other citizens flew to the ISS. But I was the first—and it cost me a cool $20 million!
It was a real once-in-a-lifetime experience! We must be on our way. Thank you, Dennis!

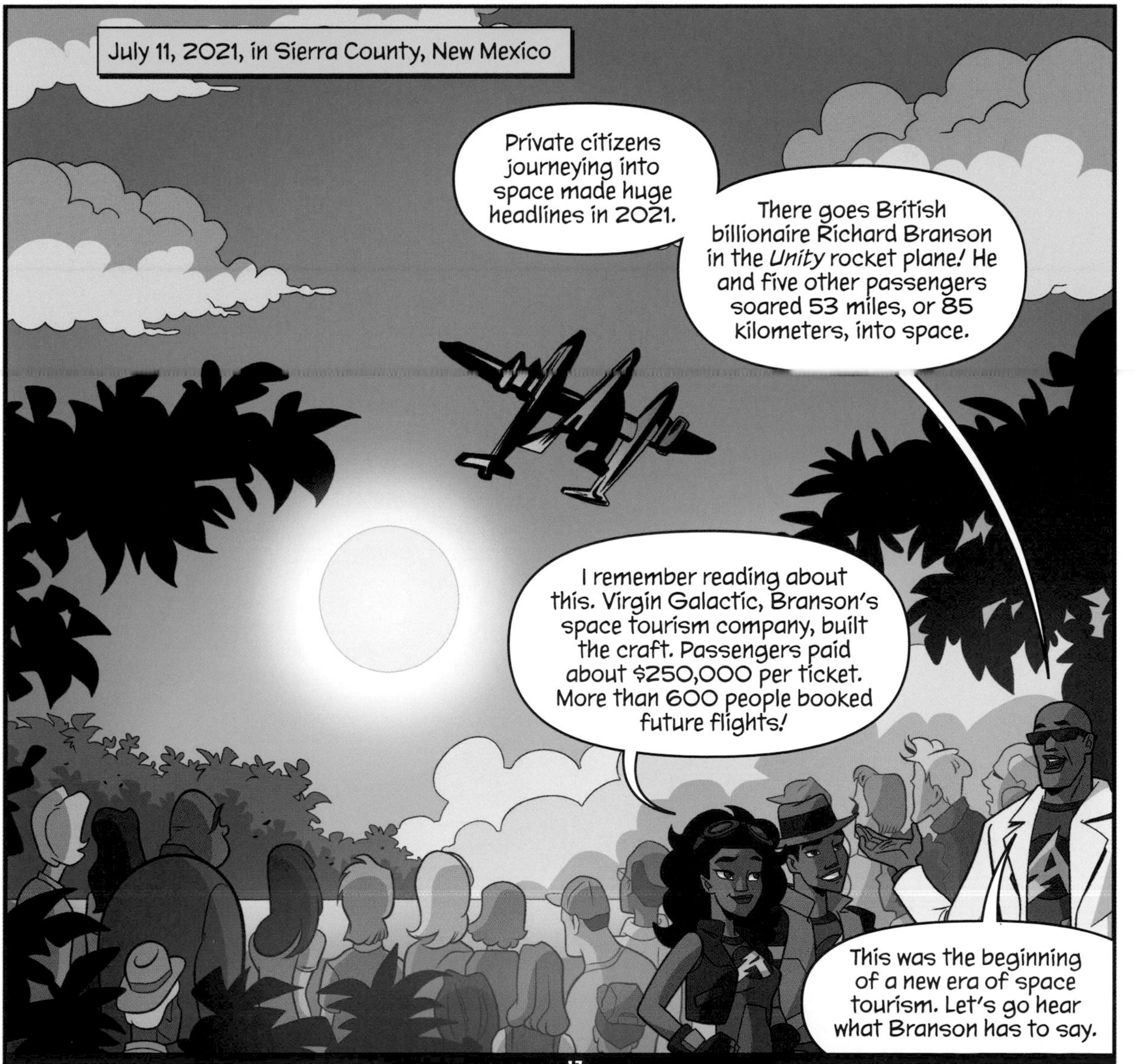
July 11, 2021, in Sierra County, New Mexico
Private citizens journeying into space made huge headlines in 2021.
There goes British billionaire Richard Branson in the *Unity* rocket plane! He and five other passengers soared 53 miles, or 85 kilometers, into space.
I remember reading about this. Virgin Galactic, Branson's space tourism company, built the craft. Passengers paid about $250,000 per ticket. More than 600 people booked future flights!
This was the beginning of a new era of space tourism. Let's go hear what Branson has to say.

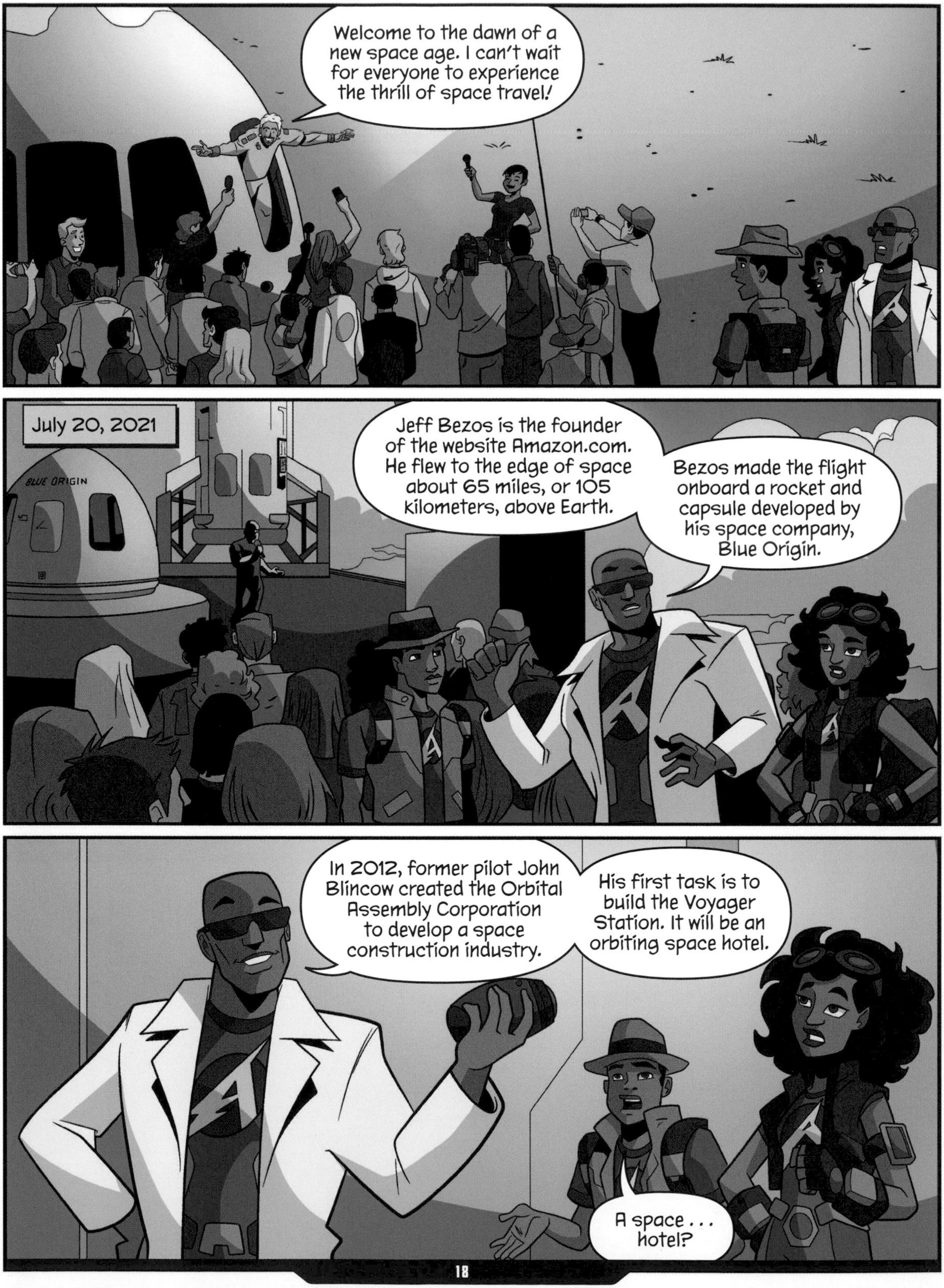

Welcome to the dawn of a new space age. I can't wait for everyone to experience the thrill of space travel!
July 20, 2021
BLUE ORIGIN
Jeff Bezos is the founder of the website Amazon.com. He flew to the edge of space about 65 miles, or 105 kilometers, above Earth.
Bezos made the flight onboard a rocket and capsule developed by his space company, Blue Origin.
In 2012, former pilot John Blincow created the Orbital Assembly Corporation to develop a space construction industry.
His first task is to build the Voyager Station. It will be an orbiting space hotel.
A space . . . hotel?

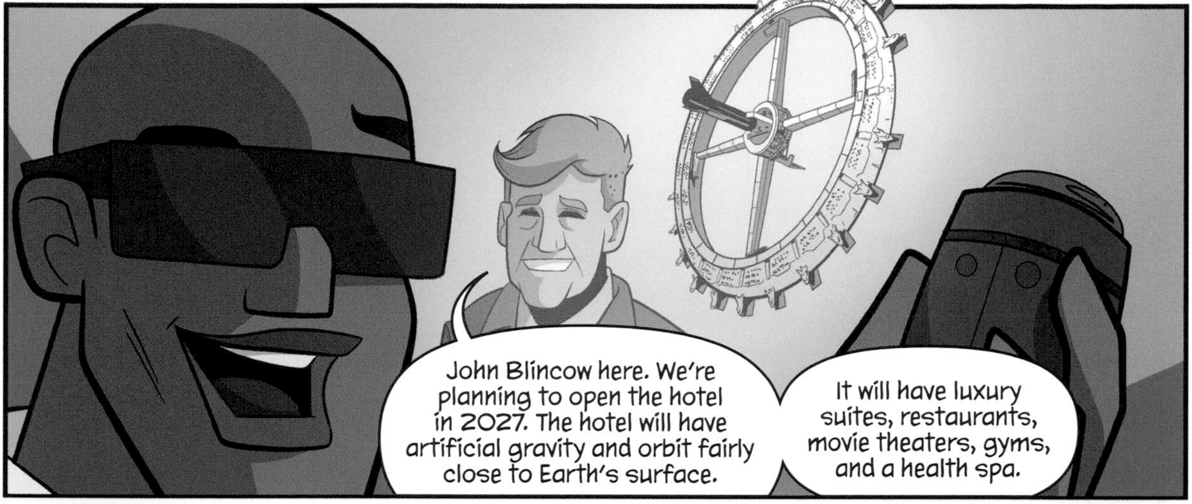
John Blincow here. We're planning to open the hotel in 2027. The hotel will have artificial gravity and orbit fairly close to Earth's surface.
It will have luxury suites, restaurants, movie theaters, gyms, and a health spa.

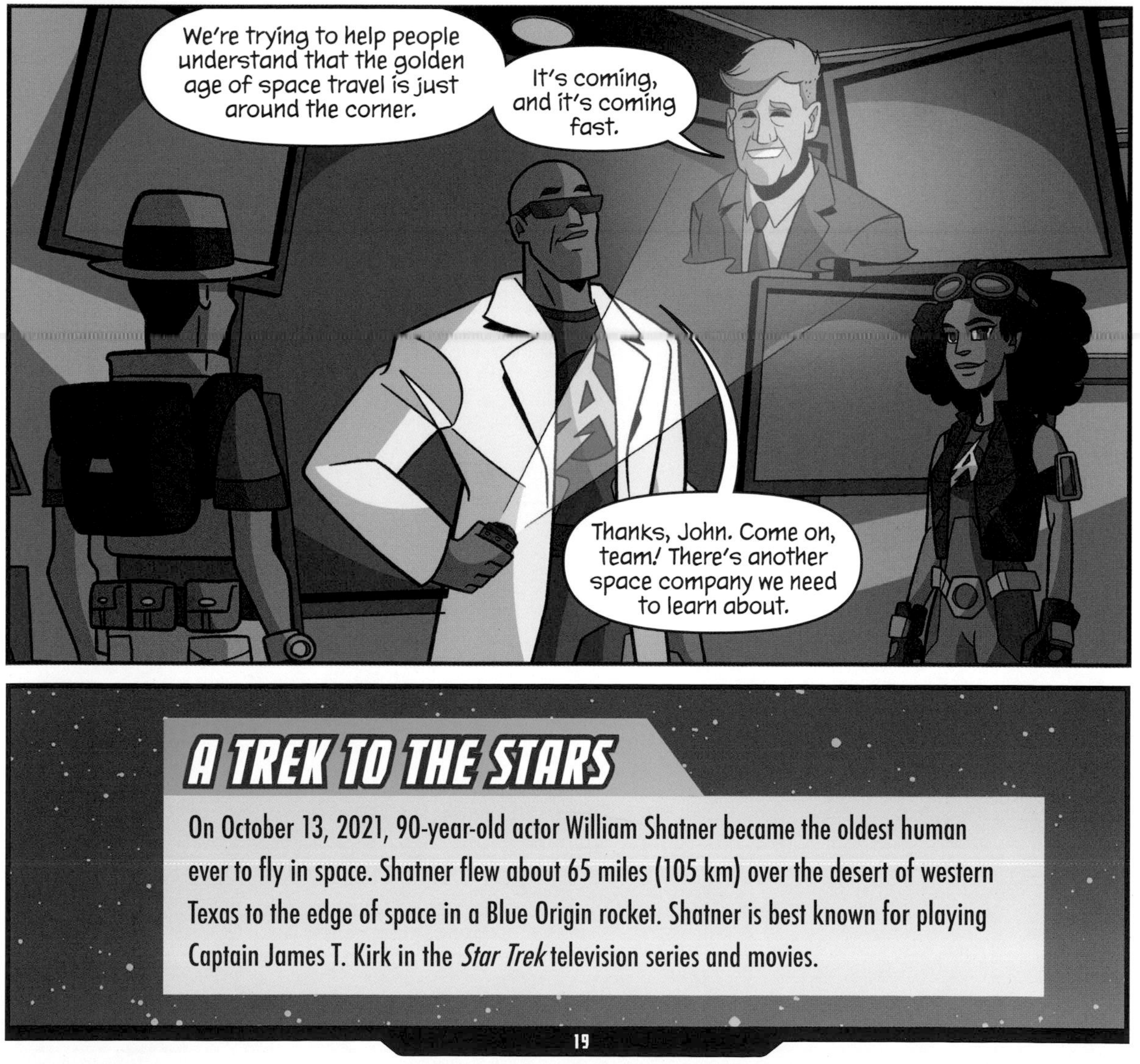
We're trying to help people understand that the golden age of space travel is just around the corner.
It's coming, and it's coming fast.
Thanks, John. Come on, team! There's another space company we need to learn about.

A TREK TO THE STARS

On October 13, 2021, 90-year-old actor William Shatner became the oldest human ever to fly in space. Shatner flew about 65 miles (105 km) over the desert of western Texas to the edge of space in a Blue Origin rocket. Shatner is best known for playing Captain James T. Kirk in the *Star Trek* television series and movies.

SECTION 4: *FUTURE COLONISTS*

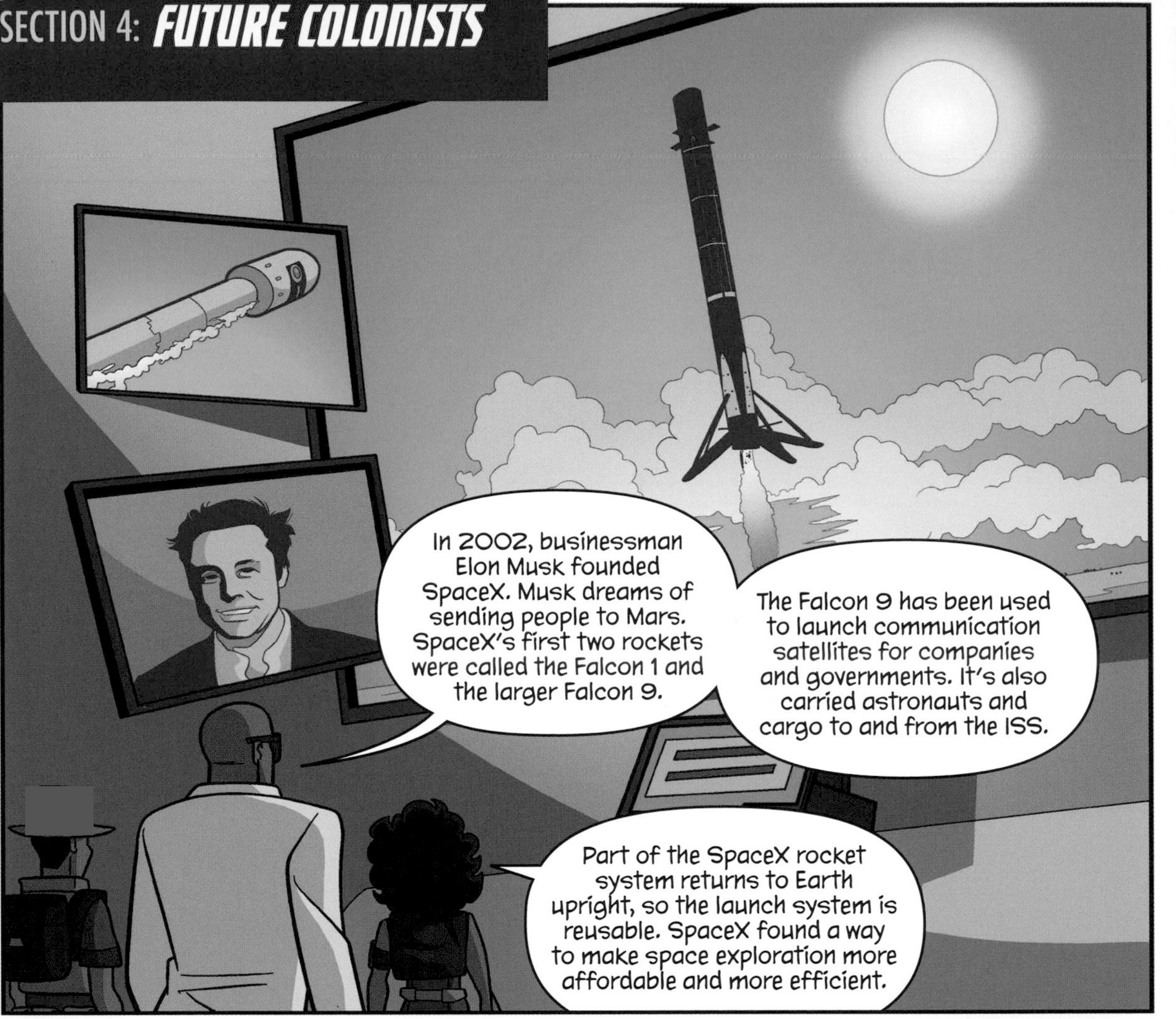
In 2002, businessman Elon Musk founded SpaceX. Musk dreams of sending people to Mars. SpaceX's first two rockets were called the Falcon 1 and the larger Falcon 9.
The Falcon 9 has been used to launch communication satellites for companies and governments. It's also carried astronauts and cargo to and from the ISS.
Part of the SpaceX rocket system returns to Earth upright, so the launch system is reusable. SpaceX found a way to make space exploration more affordable and more efficient.

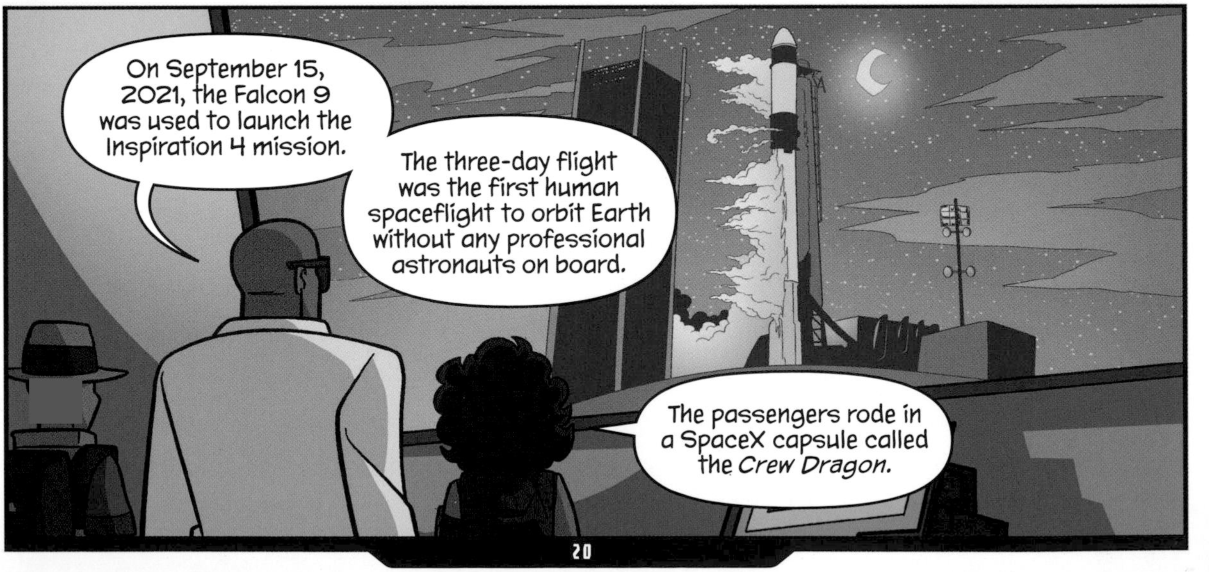
On September 15, 2021, the Falcon 9 was used to launch the Inspiration 4 mission.
The three-day flight was the first human spaceflight to orbit Earth without any professional astronauts on board.
The passengers rode in a SpaceX capsule called the *Crew Dragon*.

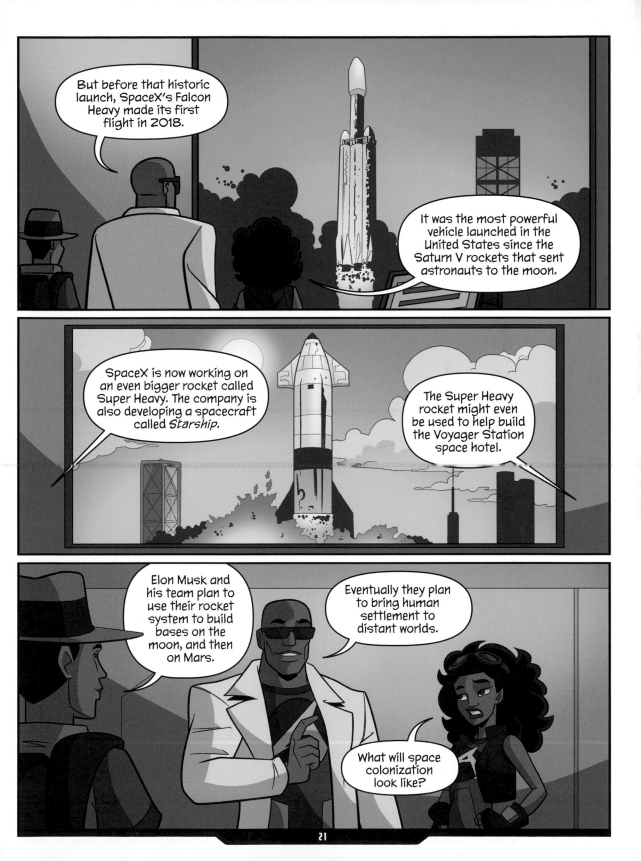

But before that historic launch, SpaceX's Falcon Heavy made its first flight in 2018.

It was the most powerful vehicle launched in the United States since the Saturn V rockets that sent astronauts to the moon.

SpaceX is now working on an even bigger rocket called Super Heavy. The company is also developing a spacecraft called *Starship*.

The Super Heavy rocket might even be used to help build the Voyager Station space hotel.

Elon Musk and his team plan to use their rocket system to build bases on the moon, and then on Mars.

Eventually they plan to bring human settlement to distant worlds.

What will space colonization look like?

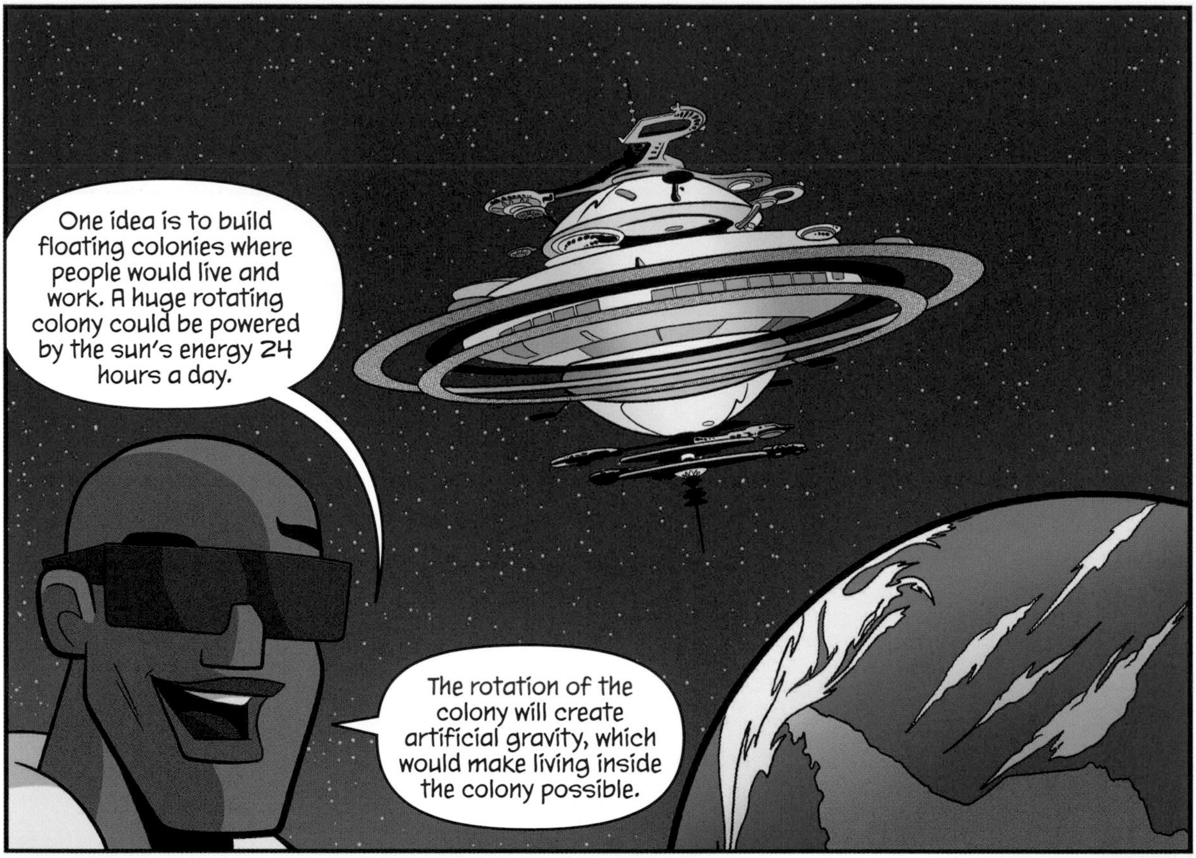
One idea is to build floating colonies where people would live and work. A huge rotating colony could be powered by the sun's energy 24 hours a day.
The rotation of the colony will create artificial gravity, which would make living inside the colony possible.

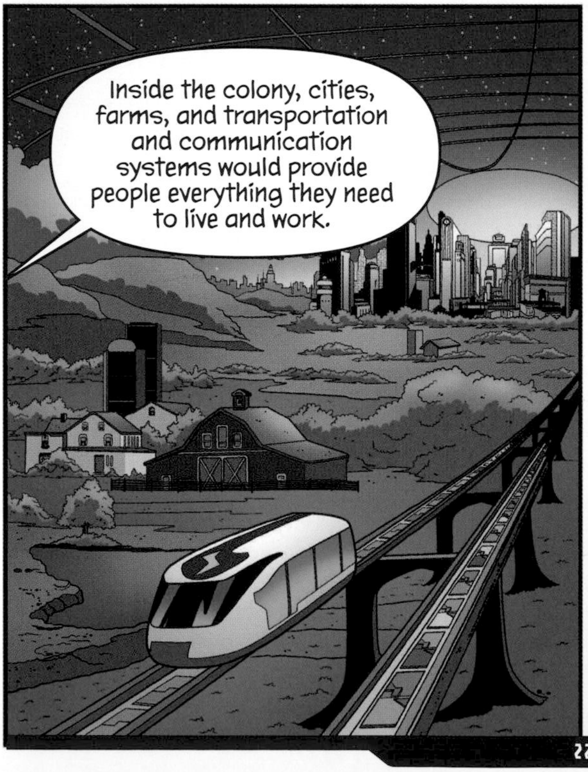
Inside the colony, cities, farms, and transportation and communication systems would provide people everything they need to live and work.

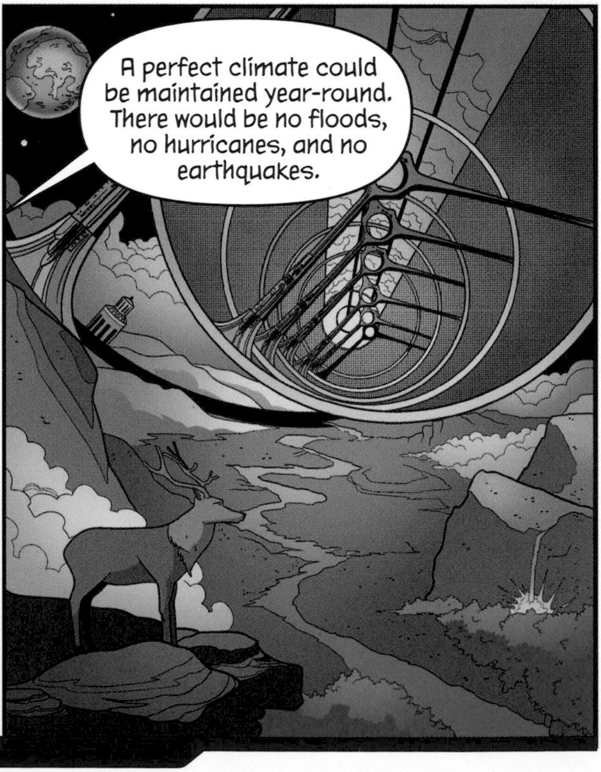
A perfect climate could be maintained year-round. There would be no floods, no hurricanes, and no earthquakes.

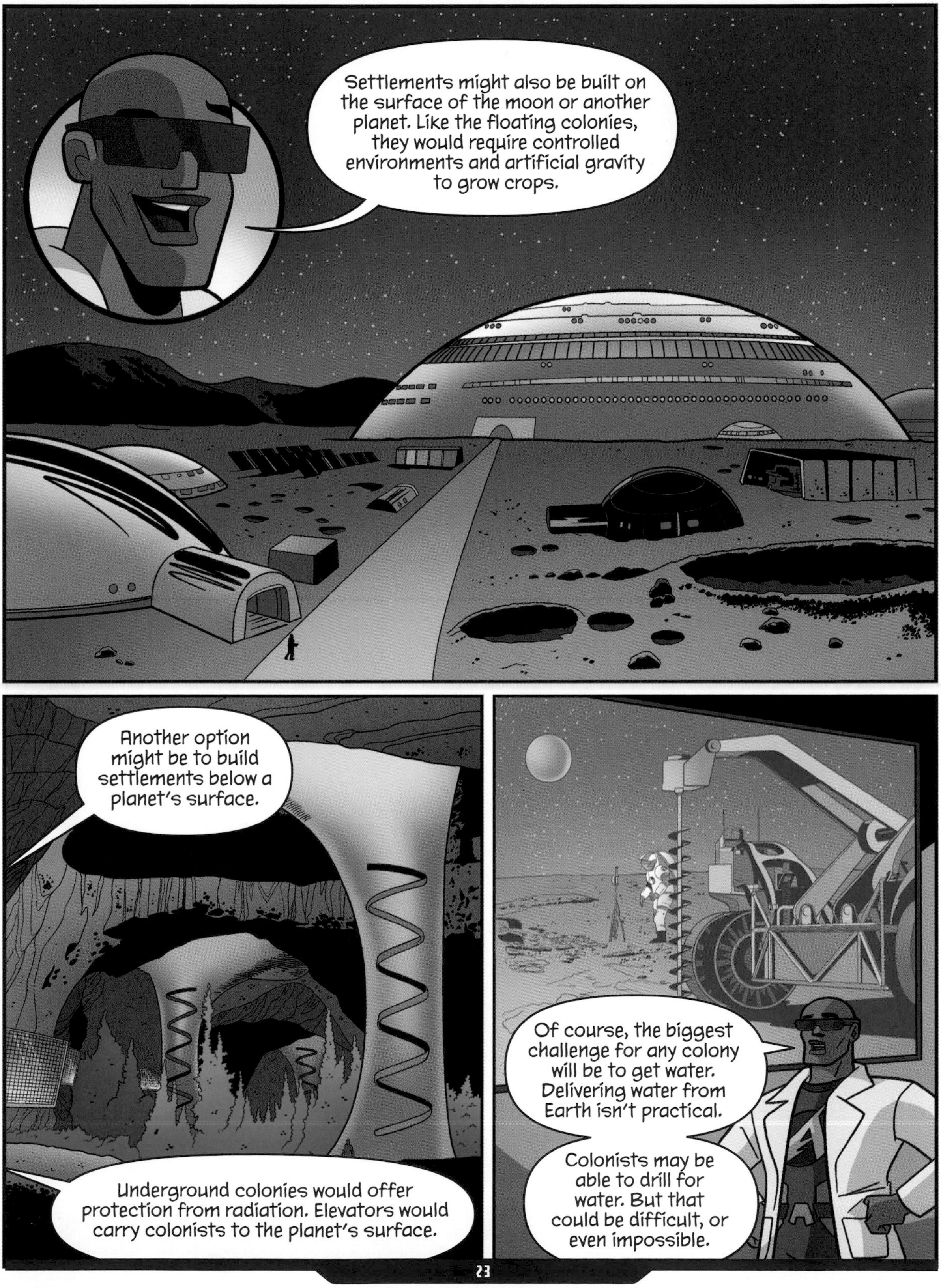
Settlements might also be built on the surface of the moon or another planet. Like the floating colonies, they would require controlled environments and artificial gravity to grow crops.
Another option might be to build settlements below a planet's surface.
Underground colonies would offer protection from radiation. Elevators would carry colonists to the planet's surface.
Of course, the biggest challenge for any colony will be to get water. Delivering water from Earth isn't practical.
Colonists may be able to drill for water. But that could be difficult, or even impossible.

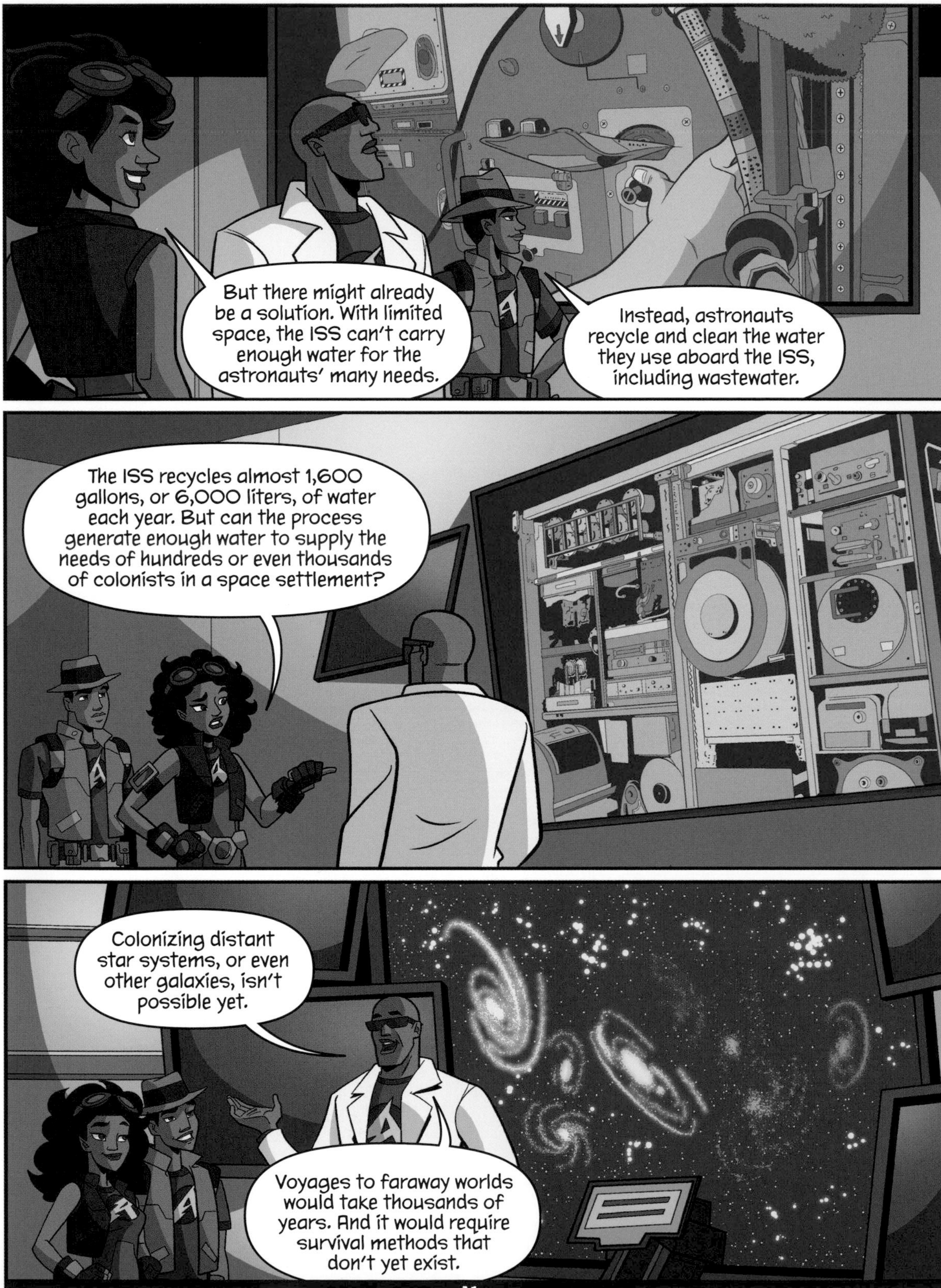

But there might already be a solution. With limited space, the ISS can't carry enough water for the astronauts' many needs.
Instead, astronauts recycle and clean the water they use aboard the ISS, including wastewater.
The ISS recycles almost 1,600 gallons, or 6,000 liters, of water each year. But can the process generate enough water to supply the needs of hundreds or even thousands of colonists in a space settlement?
Colonizing distant star systems, or even other galaxies, isn't possible yet.
Voyages to faraway worlds would take thousands of years. And it would require survival methods that don't yet exist.

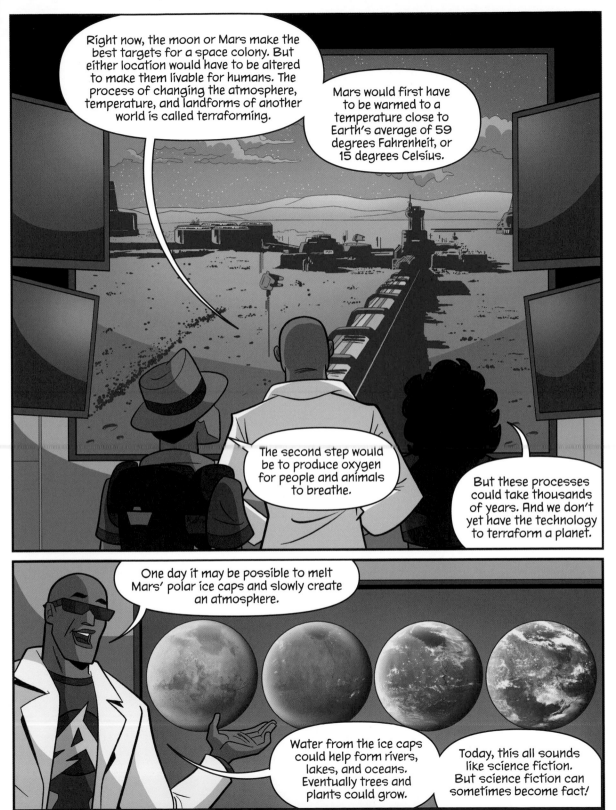

Right now, the moon or Mars make the best targets for a space colony. But either location would have to be altered to make them livable for humans. The process of changing the atmosphere, temperature, and landforms of another world is called terraforming.

Mars would first have to be warmed to a temperature close to Earth's average of 59 degrees Fahrenheit, or 15 degrees Celsius.

The second step would be to produce oxygen for people and animals to breathe.

But these processes could take thousands of years. And we don't yet have the technology to terraform a planet.

One day it may be possible to melt Mars' polar ice caps and slowly create an atmosphere.

Water from the ice caps could help form rivers, lakes, and oceans. Eventually trees and plants could grow.

Today, this all sounds like science fiction. But science fiction can sometimes become fact!

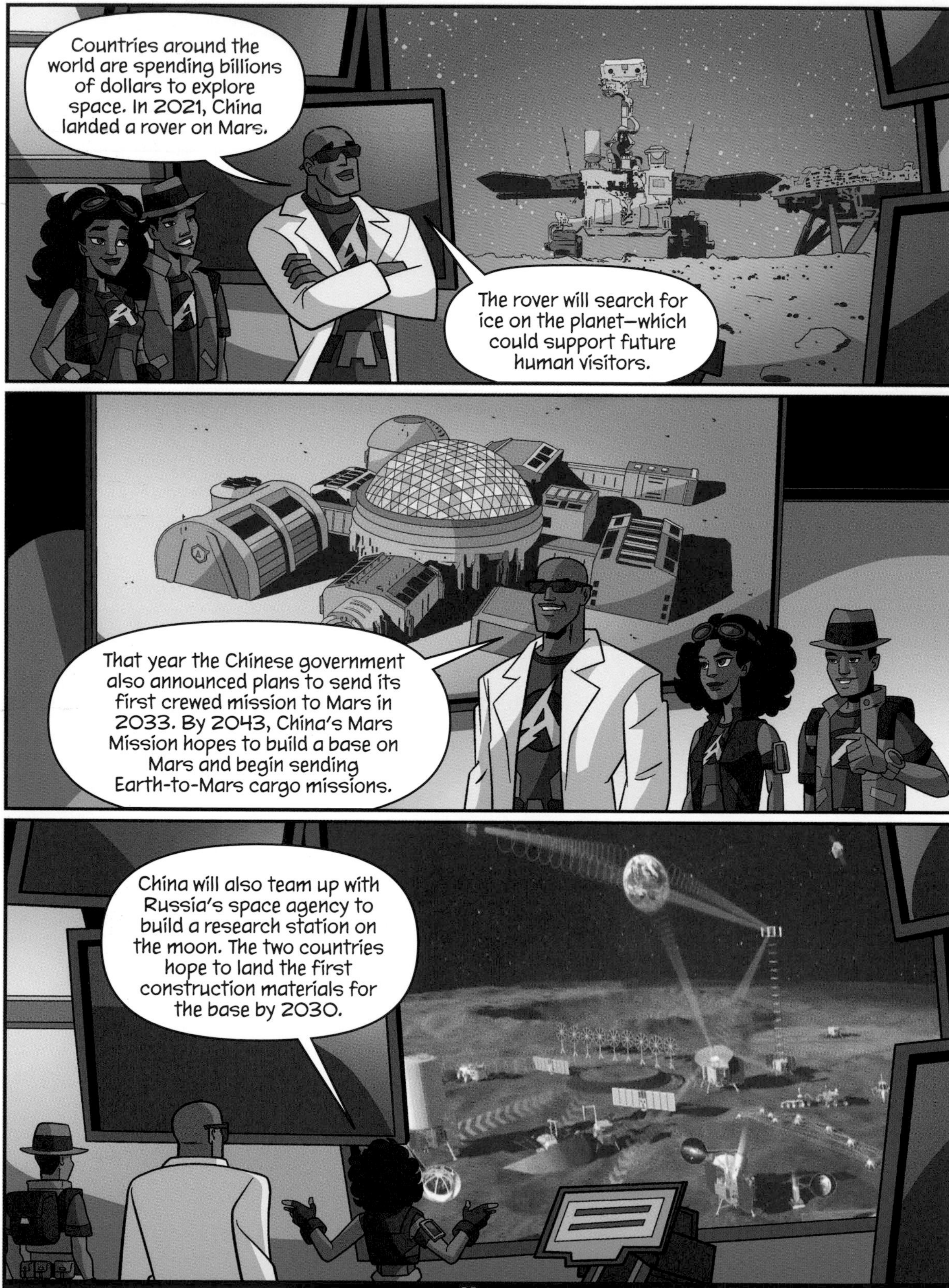
Countries around the world are spending billions of dollars to explore space. In 2021, China landed a rover on Mars.
The rover will search for ice on the planet—which could support future human visitors.
That year the Chinese government also announced plans to send its first crewed mission to Mars in 2033. By 2043, China's Mars Mission hopes to build a base on Mars and begin sending Earth-to-Mars cargo missions.
China will also team up with Russia's space agency to build a research station on the moon. The two countries hope to land the first construction materials for the base by 2030.

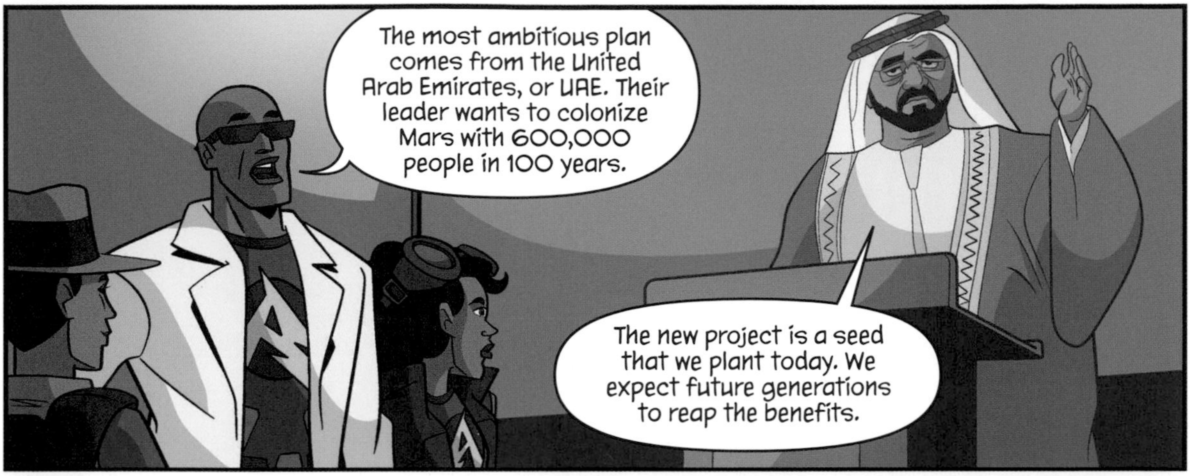
The most ambitious plan comes from the United Arab Emirates, or UAE. Their leader wants to colonize Mars with 600,000 people in 100 years.
The new project is a seed that we plant today. We expect future generations to reap the benefits.

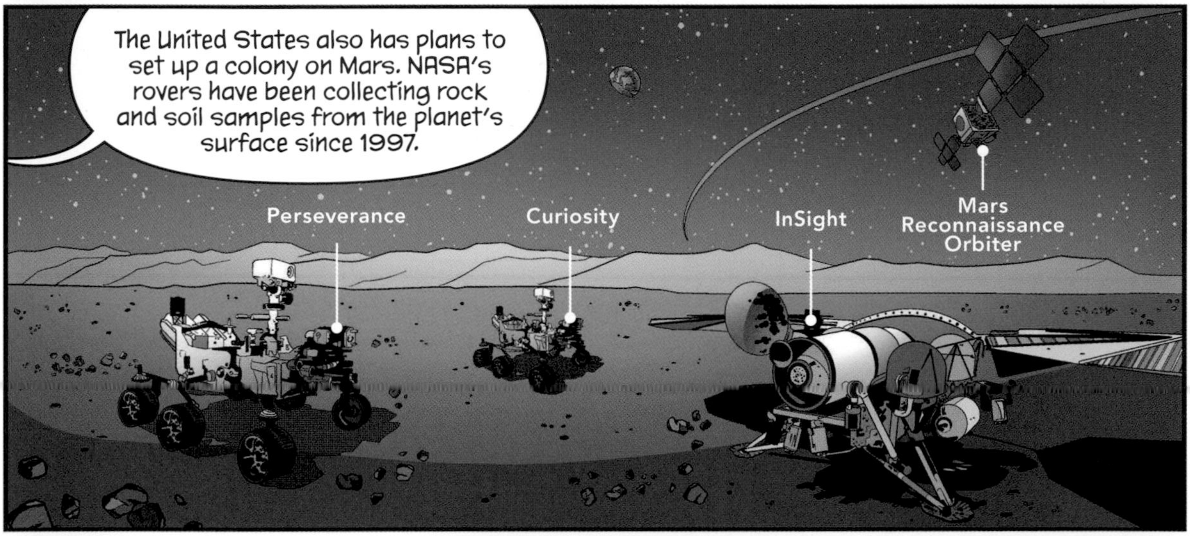
The United States also has plans to set up a colony on Mars. NASA's rovers have been collecting rock and soil samples from the planet's surface since 1997.
Perseverance
Curiosity
InSight
Mars Reconnaissance Orbiter

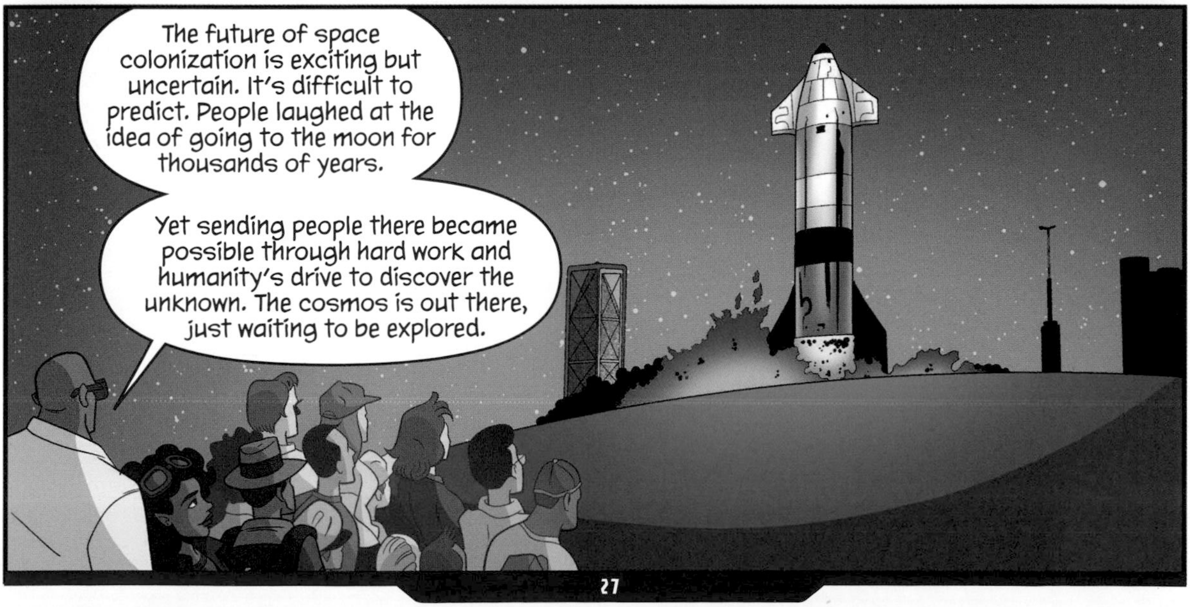
The future of space colonization is exciting but uncertain. It's difficult to predict. People laughed at the idea of going to the moon for thousands of years.
Yet sending people there became possible through hard work and humanity's drive to discover the unknown. The cosmos is out there, just waiting to be explored.

THE FUTURE OF SPACE EXPLORATION

The International Space Station (ISS) was launched and began service in 1998. The station has provided scientists with great understanding about space travel. However, after more than 20 years in operation, the ISS is getting old and its parts are wearing out. Scientists fear the station is reaching the point where it may soon be unsafe for astronauts. When its end comes, the ISS will be taken out of its orbit into an area above the southern Indian Ocean called Point Nemo. As the ISS reenters Earth's atmosphere, the intense heat and pressure will destroy most of the satellite. Debris that is not destroyed will fall harmlessly into the ocean.

SpaceX's Falcon Heavy is made of three Falcon 9 engine systems joined together to make one huge rocket. The Falcon Heavy's 27 rocket engines can generate more power than 18 747 jumbo jets. A February 2018 test launch of Falcon Heavy carried Elon Musk's personal Tesla Roadster car past Mars and into orbit around the sun. The car is worth about $100,000. Elon Musk is the founder and chief officer of Tesla, Inc.

The crew of Inspiration 4 included a physician assistant, a college professor, and a data engineer. The crew was led by Jared Isaacman, a 38-year-old billionaire who helped pay for the trip. One of the main goals of the mission was to raise money through public donations for the St. Jude's children's research hospital. The fundraising effort brought in more than $200 million.

JOURNEYING TO THE STARS

Traveling between different star systems is called interstellar travel. Right now, this type of space travel is the stuff of science fiction. However, many scientists believe interstellar travel and colonization may be possible. But can it be done?

The challenges of traveling between the stars are huge. The biggest problem is distance. Currently, our fastest space probes would take nearly 80,000 years to reach the nearest star. To reach very distant stars, humans will need new technology and massive sources of energy. One idea is to use nuclear-powered rockets that can outperform current spacecraft. Another suggestion is to harness the power of the sun. A spacecraft could use a large mirror, known as a solar sail, to capture sunlight and convert it to usable energy.

Many people believe that distance, speed, and the incredible cost make interstellar travel impossible. Yet with each new spacecraft that's built, new technologies give us greater understanding about exploring space. Human beings aren't ready for interstellar travel yet. But if we keep dreaming, perhaps one day we'll be able to reach the most distant stars.

GLOSSARY

anxiety (ang-ZYE-uh-tee)—a feeling of worry or fear often caused by a dangerous or uncertain situation

asteroid (AS-tuh-royd)—a large space rock that travels around the sun

colonize (KAH-luh-nyze)—to send a group of settlers to a new place to live and work

cosmonaut (KAHZ-muh-nawt)—a Russian astronaut

cosmos (KOZ-mohs)—the universe

module (MAH-jool)—a separate unit that can be joined to others to make a larger object such as spacecraft or machines

pandemic (pan-DEM-ik)—an outbreak of a disease that affects many people over a very large region or the whole world

radiation (ray-dee-AY-shuhn)—tiny particles that are sent out from a radioactive source

recreational (rek-ree-AY-shuhn-uhl)—when something is done for enjoyment rather than working

rover (ROH-vur)—a small vehicle used for exploring the surface of a moon or planet

satellite (SAT-uh-lyte)—a spacecraft that circles Earth, a moon, or a planet used to gather and send information

READ MORE

Bearce, Stephanie. *This or That Questions About Space and Beyond: You Decide!* North Mankato, MN: Capstone Press, 2021.

Collins, Ailynn. *Mars or Bust!: Orion and the Mission to Deep Space.* North Mankato, MN: Capstone Press, 2019.

Hubbard, Ben. *The Complete Guide to Space Exploration: A Journey of Discovery Across the Universe.* Oakland, CA: Lonely Planet, 2020.

INTERNET SITES

Colonization of Mars Facts for Kids
kids.kiddle.co/Colonization_of_Mars

Curious Kids: Can People Colonize Mars?
theconversation.com/curious-kids-can-people-colonize-mars-122251

History of Space Travel
kids.nationalgeographic.com/space/article/history-of-space-travel

Space
timeforkids.com/g56/topics/space/

INDEX

ABOUT THE AUTHOR

Nel Yomtov is a writer of children's nonfiction books and graphic novels. He specializes in writing about history, science, sports, military history, biography, and architecture. Nel has written frequently for Capstone, including two recent titles in the Movements and Resistance series. Nel lives in the New York City area.